COMING WORLD CHANGES

COMING WORLD CHANGES

BY

HARRIETTE AUGUSTA CURTISS

AND

F. HOMER CURTISS, B.S., M.D.

Founders of *The Order of Christian Mystics*

Authors of

"The Voice of Isis," "The Message of Aquaria," "The Key to the Universe," "The Key of Destiny," "Realms of the Living Dead," "Letters from the Teacher," Vols. i and ii, "Gems of Mysticism," "The Temple of Silence," "The Divine Mother," "The Philosophy of War," etc., etc.

Members of

The American Association for the Advancement of Science; The American Society for Psychical Research; The American Asiatic Association; The Authors' League of America; The League of American Pen-Women; Council of International Advisers, Optimist International; Committee on Psychology, World Conference on Narcotic Education; National Council of American Indians; The Anthony Foundation, etc., etc.

PRINTED IN THE USA

CONTENTS

FOREWORD

"Quench not the Spirit. Despise not prophesyings."
I Thessalonians, v, 19-20.

"To whom shall I speak, and give warning, that they may hear? behold, their ear is uncircumcised, and they cannot hearken: behold, the word of the Lord is unto them a reproach; they have no delight in it." *Jeremiah*, vi, 10.

While it takes a certain amount of courage to place predictions as to coming events before the people of this materialistic and skeptical age, nevertheless we would not be true to our trust unless we gave out that which has been revealed to us. It should be remembered, however, that the mere predicting of coming events does not constitute a prophet; for a prophet is "one who speaks by divine inspiration as the interpreter through whom a divinity declares himself . . . one who interprets the will of the gods to man," and prediction alone plays but a small part in his life and work. "In the *New Testament*, Christian prophets were recognized in the church as possessing a charism or spiritual gift distinct from that of ordinary teachers, and as uttering special revelations and predictions." [1]

As to the value of such prophecies at the present time we quote the following from an editorial by a prominent authority on the subject: "Since a proportion of the sensitives of our time are apparently agreed that a

[1] *The Century Dictionary.*

period of tribulation lies ahead, the question naturally arises whether these shadows of coming events serve any purpose other than to arouse emotions of fear and apprehension. . . . My own impression, for what it is worth, is that such foreshadowings have as definite a value as have those premonitory dreams to which certain individuals are liable. They afford at least an opportunity of mitigating the severity of the coming shock, and in some instances actually offer a means of avoiding the threatened crash. Much, of course, depends upon the nature of the foreshadowed crisis. Where the circumstances admit of the intervention of the free and unfettered will of the individual or individuals concerned, it is frequently possible at the critical moment to entirely avert the disaster. . . . Some of my readers will also recall the record published . . . describing how a lady was saved from embarking on the ill-fated *Lusitania* by a premonitory vision. . . . The point of this digression is that prophecies or premonitions may be turned to good account *even in cases where the outcome is inevitable.* Such forewarnings may be regarded in the light of *opportunities for the correct orientation of the inner life.* Assuming that the world is indeed destined to pass through a period of special tribulation in face of which mankind may stand impotent and helpless, there still remains to the individual freedom to meet the future either in a spirit of rebellion, or with resignation, if not with willing acceptance." [2]

[2] Editorial in *The Occult Review,* London, June, 1926.

Our object in presenting this volume to the public is not, as one mistaken reader expressed it, "to scare people into 'being good' as they used to do with the doctrine of hell fire," but to arouse them to the importance of uniting on a definite method by which the coming disasters can be minimized and "the days of tribulation" be shortened. None of the prophecies quoted from other sources give any solution or suggest any remedy or method of salvation, only the destructive aspect being presented. This has a tendency to arouse a sense of helplessness and hopeless fear, with no remedy in sight. On the contrary, in this volume *we present the constructive side and give a definite remedy* and method of salvation. We make it clear that the pessimistic outlook is not the only side of the picture. There is also an optimistic one, but its manifestation depends upon the voluntary efforts of awakened humanity.

Our readers are not urged to "be good" or even to use proved constructive methods merely to save themselves from suffering or even to save their own lives—for their past Karma and that which they generate now by heeding the warnings, following the directions and fulfilling the Law will take care of that—but they are urged to act not from personal and selfish motives, but from impersonal and unselfish motives, *i.e.*, to make themselves one of the Elect and help to generate such powerful currents of definitely constructive, radio-active, spiritual force as will counteract the destructive forces and save, not only themselves, but the great mass of unawakened and unthinking humanity whose motto seems to be, "Let us eat, drink and be merry, lest to-morrow we die."

We cannot shorten the days of tribulation by ourselves or we would have done so long ago, but the mass-force of many individuals and groups scattered over the world and working along the known psychological and spiritual laws expounded herein, *can shorten these days*. Our duty is done when we have given the Message revealed to us. With the results we have nothing to do: they depend upon humanity's reaction to the Message.

As one of our reviewers has said: [3]

"But, some one objects, we no longer believe in prophets, or the power of prophecy. . . . In the face of such skepticism, it requires a special kind of courage to put on the robes of prophet and announce a dream. Isaiah, in the *patois* of our streets, could get away with it, but a man who would imitate him to-day must do so at the risk of ridicule, contumely, and open suspicion. I therefore credit my good friends, Harriette Augusta Curtiss and her husband, F. Homer Curtiss, B.S., M.D., with very special courage, for publishing to the world their altogether astonishing dream of the future. . . .

"*They have dared to prophesy.* They have dared to reaffirm the ancient dignity and authority of prophecy. . . . The basis on which they build these prophecies

[3] Elliston A. Douglass in the *National Pictorial Monthly,* New York.

may be called naïve. Their conclusions may be assailed as emperic and unscientific. Yet, reading their simple phrasing, sensing their calm earnestness, *one is disposed to think upon what they have said. . . .* Their writings abound in thousands of minor deductions as to what the future holds—and *through them all runs the steady note of honest counsel, of deep conviction as to the responsibilities which man must assume. . . .*"

"Dr. and Mrs. Curtiss are noted internationally for the profound scholarship with which they have studied the problems of ancient and modern mysticism. Through their other books—notably *The Voice of Isis, The Message of Aquaria* and *The Key to the Universe*—they have placed some astonishing interpretations on old doctrines. Often they have challenged the most cherished superstitions of modern religion. They are entirely frank, and utterly fearless."

"Now, in their latest book, they do more than this. They picture the overturn of many a prized institution, in the coming new day. This might be termed the theme from which they have written:

"'The fetus of the New Humanity is already stirring in the Womb of Time, and, like the human mother, humanity must learn to eliminate its waste materials and poisons and give the fetus proper nourishment or the life of both the child and the mother will be endangered, as in cases of eclampsia. This is the work of the present transitory conditions. The entire thought and aim of to-day should be to meet present-day conditions as they confront us, but meet them with an intelligent conception of the advanced conditions in humanity and its organization toward which the present-day events are tending.' "

"From this angle they have approached their topic; *not for the sensation they might create* by picturing the future, but *to prepare the minds* of those who follow the philosophy of such teachings, for the changes which are at hand.

"Before outlining the predictions which Dr. and Mrs. Curtiss have made, let us see upon what they base their claim for the authority for such predictions.

"It is the contention of the authors—and also of thousands of such teachers through all the march of the centuries—that thoughts are things; actually physical entities, created by the brain as the child is created by another physical process. From this theory came the old saying, 'Coming events cast their shadows before!' Those who accept this theory contend that these thoughts work out an astral, or thought-pattern, before they ever manifest in actual happenings. . . .

"It is their contention that we are standing before the mighty portals, waiting for the curtain of time to rise on the new age, wherein wonders greater than the radio will seem commonplace to the eyes of our descendants.

"If all this seems but the fevered dream of an enthusiast, stop and consider for a moment our present position, as contrasted with that of our grandparents a hundred years ago.

"The fact that *they predicted the World War*, in a volume *published two years before* the assassination at Serajevo, lends special value to their extraordinary dream of the approaching new era in the world."

The first, and part of the fourth chapter of this volume is a collection of the prophecies of others: the balance of the book is our own.

THE AUTHORS.

Washington, D. C.
July 15, 1926.

COMING WORLD CHANGES

COMING WORLD CHANGES

CHAPTER I

THE PROPHECIES

"There shall be great tribulation, such as was not since the beginning of the world to this time." *St. Matthew,* xxiv, 21.

"God is our refuge and strength, a very present help in trouble. *Therefore will we not fear,* though the earth be removed, and though the mountains be carried into the midst of the sea." *Psalms,* xlvi, 1-2.

"Beloved of Christ, keep your star shining bright
Out through the darkness of Earth's dreary night.
'Mid toil and confusion of battle and strife,
Send your message of Love. It is life."
Harriette Augusta Curtiss in *Realms of the Living Dead,* 176.

The many prophecies as to impending disasters of cataclysmic proportions which have been given out from various sources in recent years have focused on this subject the attention of large groups of thoughtful persons who give serious consideration to the many remarkable signs of the times in which we are living. And in answer to the questions of our students in many parts of the world as to the teachings of *The Order of Christian Mystics* on the subject we will try to explain the scientific and philosophical principles underlying cataclysmic phenomena.

While we do not wish to be classed as calamity prophets, crying disaster and offering no hope or remedy—*for we here present a definite remedy*—nevertheless we consider it our duty to do all we can to warn humanity that unless the practical failure of the Locarno treaty—through the secret and petty intrigues of certain nations selfishly seeking minor advantages—is speedily counteracted, the most serious consequences will result. That agreement and accord was about the last chance for Europe to generate spiritual forces of accord and harmony which would mitigate the severity of that which is destined to occur. But first let us summarize, as briefly as possible, some of the more striking and important prophecies.

Last September Sir Arthur Conan Doyle announced [1] that for the past three years he had received repeated warnings from reliable sources in the invisible realms concerning the near approach of widespread cataclysms of so serious a nature as to impel him to warn the people of Great Britain and Europe that, "In order to arouse the world to a sense of its responsibility a great catastrophe, shattering in its nature, is approaching." He pointed out that the world had been getting into a shocking state of materialism; that the War, the Bolshevik régime, and even the epidemic diseases which have swept the world since the War, are part of the price mankind has had to pay for its sins. "The time is not certain, although everything points to its being very close. Dates are given in certain messages ranging from 1925 to 1928. If the High Powers find that

[1] *London Morning Post*, Sept. 17, 1925.

mankind is improving, and that the world can be cleansed and brought by other means to its right mind as regards strict spiritual matters, then we may be saved." In conclusion Sir Arthur added that confirmatory messages were being received from all parts of the world, but that the subject should not be treated as a sensation.

In a personal letter to the Authors, under the date of April 18, 1926, Sir Arthur says:

"We still get incessant messages of coming trouble—short, sharp and salutary. By 'short' I mean about three years. Always it is to end in a great psychic demonstration corresponding with the second coming, which will show the world how mad it has been in its stupid and obstinate rejection of the advances from the higher world. Each nation will suffer according to the extent of that rejection, and the 'Elect' whom you quote will be those who have worked for this cause. In that hour of tribulation Nations will realize what they owe to those who have obscured the light . . . but when it is to occur—beyond a general sense of nearness—or how far some spiritual change in us may modify or even stop it is more than I can say. My impression is that it is too far gone for that. I have about 100,000 words of detail . . ."

On November 25, 1922, Mary Forbes—a prophetess of Boston who has spent most of her life in India studying Oriental mysticism, and who gained widespread attention by her accurate prophecy of the World War two years before it began—predicted, "A great war by the Orient against the Occident. The East will win. Violent earthquakes will destroy most of Europe, except parts of France and Russia. A new continent will arise in the Pacific." [2]

"Terror-stricken by prophecies of the world's end in 1926 made by Enoch, prophet of the Mexican people in Nogales, Sonora, hundreds of residents of the Mexican border town to-day began religious preparations for 'the end.' Enoch said the coming year will be a succession of tremors over the earth. Cities will be leveled and the loss of life will be tremendous, he predicted. As the earthquakes subside, he prophesied, a terrible heat will settle upon the earth and dry places will ignite." [3]

Showing that such prophecies are not confined to the prophets of the Western world we find a similar prophecy coming from far-off China. "The Chinese throughout the Philippines are busy building rafts on which to escape from a world catastrophe, prophecies of which have roused a panic that is seriously affecting business. *The Society for the Unification of the World's Religions*, at Chengtu, Szechwan, China, announces, first, a great earthquake, spreading to all lands at the same moment; second, a great eclipse, affecting both Sun and Moon; third, a vast flood, caused by the overflowing of the ocean; fourth, a violent vibration in the air 1,000 times louder than any thunder; fifth, some stars becoming cracked and pieces falling upon the Earth; sixth, numerous angels descending to Earth.

[2] *San Francisco Journal,* Nov. 26, 1922.
[3] *San Francisco Chronicle,* June 4, 1925.

These prophecies are printed in Chinese characters on thin tissue paper and have caused great alarm." [4]

Reasoning from an astrological standpoint, M. D. Sagane says [5] that:

"It is an admitted fact that what are called the superior planets . . . certainly produce remarkable results by their transits taken in relation to the signs ruling particular countries. . . . In the year 1926 Neptune will be in Leo, Saturn in Scorpio and Jupiter in Aquarius, and *in squares and oppositions*—the worst possible aspects—to one another. Also Mars will be in the fixed signs Aquarius and Taurus in August and May, and August to December respectively, and will thus add to the aforesaid influences. As a result there will be gigantic convulsions and disasters after disasters in the physical—earthquakes, eruptions, floods, etc.—and political spheres. The countries that will experience these God-sent things will be Ireland, Poland, Prussia, Sweden, France, Russia, Italy, Asia Minor, Arabia and Persia. We may even expect bloodshed."

The Australian seer, Victor E. Cromer, says that:

"The next seven years are to be the most awe-inspiring that the world has ever seen. On the one hand we are to have a series of mighty cataclysms, and on the other hand events leading up to the revealing of the World Teacher and the organization of the New Age. . . . These three countries (Germany, Russia,

[4] Abstracted from an article in the *Far Eastern News*, Peking, Jan. 23, 1924.

[5] *The Kalpaka Magazine*, Dec. 1925, 558.

Turkey) will league themselves into an unholy alliance about July, 1926, and shortly afterwards a new world war will begin. . . . This war will last about four years, and will be the most terrible war in the history of the world. . . . Germany is now perfecting the 'death ray,'[6] so that she 'maketh fire to come down from heaven on the earth in the sight of men,' (*Rev.* xiii, 13) indicating the nature of the next war, an aerial campaign. . . . The pyramid measures undoubtedly answer to the various epochs of our history. And not only is the first 'low passage' an exact measure of the late Great War, at the rate of one inch per month, but the next and final low passage in the approach to the King's Chamber is an exact demarcation of the time limits of the next and final Great War which is called Armageddon, followed by the Great Desolation or Earthquake. According to all measures now in use, this period begins at the end of July, 1926. . . . It is the new measure which fulfills the prophecy concerning the 'shortening of the times' of tribulation. This measure shows the beginning to be in October of 1926 and the end in November of 1932. . . . A period of six years one month and three days . . . so that from 1926 to 1932 the world will be in tribulation 'such as never was since the beginning of the world.' But side by side with the tribulation, will be the wonderful outpouring of the Shekinah or Visible Glory of God, leading to the establishment of the New Age. . . . The 'Kings of the East' are the great Buddhist leaders of

[6] If a "death ray," then it is possible to develop a "life ray" to counteract it.

the Mongolian race who will occupy the territory after the devastation. Australia and America and whatever new land rises in the New World will be the scene of the Christian Millennium, while the Mongolian races will enjoy a Buddhist Millennium in the Old World, but they will work in perfect harmony with the New World after the New Age has started. After the trials and tribulations of the next seven years, the Great Peace will descend upon the world and the nations will learn the art of war no more. . . .

"The means by which the World Teacher will be revealed to the world will be by a remarkable outpouring of spiritual magnetism, which will surround Him with a pranic sea which will appear like a flaming fire to the vision of those who look upon Him. From the moment that this remarkable and wonderful manifestation takes place the organization of the New Age will go on by leaps and bounds. The whole world will be astounded at the mighty series of events which will take place. On the one hand there will be a mighty war raging, and on the other hand the events leading to the organization of the New Age." [7]

A profound student of the pyramid measurements, Mr. W. H. F. MacHuisdean, claims that: "The Great Tribulation is indicated in the Great Pyramid to occur in 1928 A.D."

A remarkable prophetic vision, received in full waking consciousness, has recently been published by an English mystic, Mr. E. A. Chaylor, evidently referring to the coming cataclysms:

[7] *The Kalpaka Magazine,* Jan. 1926, 11-12-13, Feb., 1926, 90-1-2.

"I saw the land (Europe) spread out below me. At the four corners stood four Men, holding each the corner of a black cloth. Now a wind came from the East, causing the cloth to billow and shake. Then I asked one of the Men, 'What is the meaning of the cloth?' And he said, *'It is the Shadow of those things about to come upon the Earth.'* Then the four Men lowered the cloth, and it covered all the land.

"The wind now blew with violence, and there was a great shaking, with clamor and confusion, and the cloth became soaked with blood. Then I asked the Man, 'Why are these things done?' And he answered me, *'Because those things which hindered are about to be removed.'* And I said, 'What are the things which are to be removed?' And again he answered me, *'They are three: the first two shall be destroyed by the third, and the third, when its work is accomplished, shall be changed!'*

"Yet again I asked him, 'How shall these things be?' And he said, *'The lands which you see have passed the Cycle of Hate; they are now in the Cycle of Madness. The next Cycle is the Cycle of Destruction.'* And I said, 'How long until this Cycle shall end?' And he answered me, *'In about two years* (1928) *it shall end, and destruction shall commence. Then, in nine years the times of nine nations shall be accomplished.'*

"Now the cloth dissolved away, and the land was seen to be desolate. The lines which had divided it were removed, and over all there was silence. Then, out of the silence was heard a Trumpet, and a Voice speaking Wisdom. And because of the silence the people heard the Voice, and thereafter, for a space there was Peace in the Land." The editor of the magazine remarks, "If there is anything in the somber vision recorded by the author . . . then the need for special effort on the part of every earnest student to contribute his quota to the efforts of the forces of light is in the highest degree imperative. . . . That the world is rapidly approaching some dire crisis the present trend of events unfortunately leaves little room for doubt." [8]

Many years ago Mme. Blavatsky wrote:

"As the sidereal motions do regulate and determine events on Earth . . . these events have to submit to predetermination by simple astronomical calculations. . . . It is simply knowledge, and mathematically correct computations, which enable the *Wise Men of the East* to foretell, for instance, that England is on the eve of such or another catastrophe; that France is nearing such a point in her Cycle; and that Europe in general is threatened with, or rather is on the eve of, a cataclysm to which her own cycle of racial Karma has led her." [9]

A leading contemporary authority on astrology [10] considered the planetary conditions to "be accountable for the greatest series of earthquakes that has ever affected the world during the period of 5,925 years past."

[8] *The Occult Review,* May, 1926, 322-3, 293-4.

[9] *The Secret Doctrine,* i, 707-8.

[10] Walter Gorn Old (Sepharial) in *The British Journal of Astrology,* Aug., 1925.

In 1914 we published[11] several remarkable prophecies received from unusual sources, among which were the following:

Prophecy of the Storm Wind

"I am the Spirit of the Storm Wind that blows the waves: that changes the day to night; that saddens the world and lets the rain from the mighty deep pour over the darkened Earth until it is engulfed.

"Blow, blow, blow, ye winds! Blow from the West, blow from the North!
"Let the ocean find itself a new bed!
"What is so beautiful as the breakers on the shore!"

An Undine's Prophecy

(The more remarkable because given in June, 1914.)

"The waters shall cleanse the Earth! The dead and dying both alike are carried away by the beautiful clear waters of the ocean.

"The implements of death, misery and suffering are all washed away, and the beautiful waters of the ocean, with the sunlight on them, are moving, moving, so calm and sweet and clean.

"Breathe in the salt air, the salt, salt air of the ocean!

"What is this putrid smell of unburied thousands? Of earth saturated with blood? What is this death that man has made? It is hideous. It smells aloud to heaven. How horrible!

[11] *Realms of the Living Dead,* Curtiss, 173-4-5.

"Then the beautiful clear waters come with their sweet breath of purity and life, the salt of purity and sweetness. Smell the air! How sweet it is!

"This is not death; for there is no death. It is only the Divine Law which goes forth and says: 'Go back and be washed by the ocean: be covered up. When purified let the dry land appear.'

"All this land will be filled with forces, little seeds of love and life that have been purified by the waters. And they draw to themselves other forces, and out of these, little flames of life try to embody themselves in trees and grass and flowers. They grow stronger and embody themselves in something else.

"After a long, long time God says to man: 'Go and dwell on the new land I have made for you.' Then man comes and finds all things growing. Then God says, 'These are the things you have made. I have sent my ocean to wash away the wickedness you created by your thoughts. But in your spirit the Divine Life centered and has brought forth."

The Spirit of the Ocean Waves

"Onward, onward we go! The ocean is king! The ocean is king!
Down, down, O land, underneath the waves!
A new day, a new place to play, ye nymphs of the caves!

"Man, puny creature, is gone. And the land where he dwelt and made his proud boast, where is it now?

Under the waves! And over it the dolphins dance and play all day.

"O puny man, where is your kingdom? Would you keep back the Great Deep? Ha! Ha!

"Onward, onward over the land! Now it is gone. The spray dashes high and the beautiful Sun shines through its depths and makes myriads of diamonds and pearls. They are not tears, but pearls, pearls of joy, joy, joy! while the dolphins dance and play. For the land is gone, is gone, is gone."

Those who base their predictions upon the prophecies of the Bible, and who are striking terror to the hearts of thousands by asserting that the coming changes mean "the end of the world," we have quite fully dealt with in the chapter on "Are These the Last Days" in our book, *The Message of Aquaria*.[12] In it we show that,

"Since all creation, as manifested in Nature and in the history of nations, follows a parallel course, these prophecies point unmistakably to the close of some great period; not 'the end of the world,' as many think, but the end of a dispensation, the end of a great cycle, in this case the end of a sub-race. . . . The coming sixth sub-race into whose beginnings humanity is now entering will not usher in the millennium referred to in the biblical prophecies, but will foreshadow and prepare for it, sow the seed, as it were. That is, there will be such a tremendous uplift and advance over previous conditions as they existed before the World War

[12] *The Message of Aquaria*, Curtiss, 40, 44.

—spiritually, mentally and physically—that to many it will seem to be the dawn of the millennium. . . . Therefore, the great importance of arousing all who will listen to a recognition of the necessity of taking advantage of the great opportunities now offered for special progress and setting out in earnest on the Path or striving to live the Mystic Life. For this is truly 'the end of the world' (cycle) for those who refuse utterly to respond to the higher ideals that are now being set forth for humanity's standard and attainment."[12]

[12] Pages 40, 44.

CHAPTER II

GEOLOGICAL CONSIDERATIONS

"That the periodical sinking and reappearance of mighty Continents, now called Atlantean and Lemurian by modern writers, is no fiction, will be demonstrated. . . . It is only in the twentieth century that portions, if not the whole, of the present work will be vindicated." *The Secret Doctrine,* Blavatsky, ii, 340, 461.

"O Souls who are patiently waiting for day,
Be not discouraged; turn not away;
For the day that is dawning is gloriously bright;
The dreams so appalling will flee with the night."
Harriette Augusta Curtiss in *Realms of the Living Dead,* 176.

Before taking up an explanation of the prophecies in detail, let us first consider an outline of what the cosmic philosophy of *The Order of Christian Mystics* teaches as to the planet as a whole. The fundamental idea to grasp is that this globe is not a mere mass of rocks and earth and seas; a mere mechanical mixture of dead and inert substances held together by purely mechanical forces. Nearly all ancient philosophers and peoples recognized that the Earth is a living entity, a gigantic organism with its own stages of growth and evolution and its own life history quite independent of, although affected by, the various classes of living creatures which dwell upon its surface and within it.

Not only is the Earth's surface in constant motion, through its daily tides of ocean and land—the height of the land-tide being estimated at 18 inches—but the entire surface undergoes a constant undulating movement of vast extent. The rate of this continental movement is so slow that it is imperceptible except as it reaches its periods of climax, when comparatively sudden readjustments of the surface take place. Ultimately this vast undulation successively raises and submerges whole continents and peoples, such as the submergence of the Hyperborean continent and the Second Great Race, the Lemurian continent and the Third Race, the Atlantean continent and the Fourth Race.[1]

Geologists recognize this cyclic elevation and submersion of continents in the character of the stratified rocks, with their various types of fossils, etc., and such discoveries as the remains of tropical vegetation in Greenland and what are now the polar regions. The point to keep in mind is that while such changes in the arrangement of the Earth's surface are cyclic, periodic and inevitable, by taking proper measures and by heeding the prophecies of their enlightened Seers, mankind can accommodate itself to such changes without serious disaster. The vital point is that while these changes are ultimately inevitable, they can take place gradually and harmoniously, giving mankind time to adapt itself to them without too great loss if they will obey their Seers, or they can take place rapidly and destructively, according as the vibration of harmony and cooperation or the vibration of inharmony, antagonism and evil is the keynote sounded by mankind as a whole.

[1] For details see chapter "The Origin of Man" in *The Voice of Isis*, Curtiss, 230.

During the winter of 1925-6 there was comparatively little snow in Alaska, and that region which formerly had a sub-polar climate has been warmer than many parts of the United States, although for the past four years the heat radiated by the Sun has been much below the normal amount. "The return of volcanic activity to North America's loftiest peak, Mount McKinley (20,300 feet), is indicative of a series of volcanic phenomena in which many observers to-day see a promise of radical and permanent climatic changes in the southern part of Alaska. Since Mt. Shishaldin, in the Aleutians 800 miles southwest of Mt. McKinley, erupted November 11, 1925, this region has experienced a springlike November and December unparalleled in the memory of the oldest inhabitant. Streams usually frozen at this season have remained open, and in place of the usual snowbound landscape there is green vegetation. The affected area covers several hundred square miles along Cook Inlet . . . and far up the valley of the Sushitna river. Anchorage had a Fahrenheit temperature of 28 degrees above on Christmas day, when the mercury is usually around zero . . . the warm air from Cook Inlet's heated waters caused considerable melting of large glaciers. Observers believe that subterranean fires are eating their way northward. . . . Geologists consider these forces similar to those which ages ago submerged the land-bridge between North America and Asia. . . . Many think the banishment of the former bitter winters from this part of Alaska may be permanent."[2]

[2] *Associated Press* dispatch, Dec. 30, 1925.

According to reports from the University of Norway, "The Arctic Ocean has been growing steadily warmer since 1918, and to-day the Arctic is not recognizable as the same region of 1868 to 1917. Where formerly there were great masses of ice, he—Captain Martin Ingebrigsten, who has sailed the Arctic for 50 years —found mountains of earth and stones. At many points well-known glaciers have entirely disappeared. The disappearance of whitefish and seals is accompanied by the appearance of vast schools of herring and also smelts, fish which have never before ventured so far North."

"The discovery of a new volcano located on the tiny Albemarle Island of the Galapagos group off the coast of Ecuador, has been officially entered in the records of the navy hydrographic office in San Francisco. The discovery was reported by Captain J. S. Collier of the Union Oil tank steamer *Montebello* which approached within half a mile of the island. . . . The volcano was pouring a stream of lava some 20 feet wide and many feet deep into the ocean, creating a shoal which the *Montebello's* skipper reported as a menace to navigation." [3]

On his recent [4] return from a two and a half years' cruise in the interests of the Cleveland Museum of Natural History, Captain George F. Simmons reported the discovery and naming of two new islands in the Martin Vas group in the South Atlantic off the coast of Brazil.

[3] *San Francisco Chronicle,* Jan. 18, 1926.
[4] June 5, 1926.

After being inactive for over five years, the violent outburst of the volcano Mauna Loa in the Hawaiian Islands on April 17, 1926, presented the most awe-inspiring spectacle in the memory of the islanders. Fountains of fire spouted 400 feet high above the crater and formed burning rivers of lava 1800 feet wide and many feet deep. The stream of lava completely engulfed the village of Hoopuloa, together with many ranches. The village and wharf were buried 50 feet deep and as the lava poured into the sea it started the water to boiling several hundred feet out to sea.

These examples are sufficient to show that practically the whole northern portion of the Pacific is in a seething condition, owing to the relatively rapid rise of the old continent of Lemuria. No wonder scientists tell us that there are six submarine quakes to one on land! Much of California, especially the chain of islands along its coast, and part of Mexico with its islands and their antediluvian animals—sea elephants, etc.—was once a part of Lemuria, later covered with a volcanic crust and volcanic sand for many miles inland. In fact, a great part of the Western coast of America, and the chain of islands all the way up to the North, was formed in this way. Hence this region is particularly apt to suffer from quakes, upheavals and tidal waves, as evidenced by the serious quake at Santa Barbara last year (1925) and the repeated minor shocks all along the coast.

But the western coast of North America and the Pacific ocean are not the only areas that are undergoing marked and often violent changes. Our attention has recently been called to the fact that "portentous significance is to be attached to other signs which . . . are of greater import as foreshadowing the onset of a crisis in the earth's history which may well bring about in the near future a vast alteration in the existing configuration of oceans and continents. These tokens . . . bear witness to the oncoming of an era of readjustment in the balance of our planet—a loss of equilibrium which . . . may yet gather force and impetus which . . . would, ere long, rush to its climax. . . . Strange are the reports of sea erosion and the disappearance of the coastline in localities near home and far remote. At Cochin we hear of such inroads so extensive and so threatening that the residents of the foreshore are moving inland. There is no explanation of the phenomena. Our own Southwestern coast (of England) is the subject of a change slower but no less sure. From Minehead, in North Devon, around the Cornish coast and along the South as far as Lancing, in Sussex, a steady advance of the sea has been noted. The action of local currents will not explain this. . . . One thing is certain, namely, that the bed of the Atlantic is rising, and rising rapidly, in certain places. . . . In the Bay of Gascony . . . there was an ocean profundity which fathomed, we understand, *two and a half miles.* At one point in this area the commander of the French transport *Loriet* found no more than 132 feet of water. Other parts of the Atlantic have also been found to be rising. . . . Ocean currents are affected, with an inevitable reaction on climate. . . . But the result of a lifting of the ocean bed must be to raise the sea-level and cause it to overflow those lands which are thus correspondingly depressed. . . . The disturbance of the ocean bed is worldwide." [5]

"After taking all the trouble to ascertain the exact position of a new island in the China Sea and mark it on the charts, the hydrographers of the various nations have had to expunge it again . . . islands, which are the tops of submarine mountains, frequently appear and disappear. . . . This island was the largest of several thrown up during the recent Japanese earthquake. When it was apparently firmly set and vegetation commenced to grow on it, one of the most notorious of the Chinese pirates, known as Mala Dahlak, settled on it with his band of desperadoes. . . . Then one day . . . they saw that Mala Dahlak and his island had utterly vanished. Subsequent investigation established the fact that where the island stood there is now twenty-five fathoms of water. . . . The rising of the Atlantic bed . . . is *one of the most vast and important of the changes in the earth's surface.* It was discovered when the Eastern Cable Company's cable between Cape Town and St. Helena broke some 800 miles north of the Cape. The repair ship, instead of finding it at the depth it was laid, in 1899, of 2,700 fathoms, or just over three miles, picked it up at only a little more than three-quarters of a mile deep. Therefore *the ocean bed must have risen more than two miles* within the last twenty-five years." [6]

As the result of purely scientific investigations we

[5] *Psychic Science,* Jan., 1926, 248.
[6] *The Literary Digest,* Jan. 31, 1925.

may mention an article published in 1922 by Dr. Milton A. Nobles, a noted geologist and authority on earthquakes and volcanoes, in which he predicted a series of disasters in an "earthquake belt" embracing the exact spots where most of the large earthquakes and volcanic eruptions occurred in the year (1923) following. In 1923 Dr. Nobles published a map in which he outlined a belt extending around the globe which embraced most of the world's active volcanoes, and which he predicted would be the scene of great cataclysmic changes during the next ten years (1923-33).

In our Prophecy from the one called the King of the World,[7] given in December, 1922, it was stated that owing to volcanic activity *and a tilting of the axis of the Earth,* vast and cataclysmic changes were to take place in the comparatively near future which would entirely remodel and rearrange the land surface of the globe. Mr. Nobles' article predicts the beginning of these changes, showing that we are not the only ones to sense the coming changes, and also showing that these predictions are not mere fanciful dreams of impractical visionaries, but have a sound scientific basis. To quote from Mr. Nobles' article:

"Southwestern Europe and the Near East of Asia are being undermined like a section of creampuff under internal pressure. This corner of the world will soon be ready to sink and make room for the surrounding waters to rush in. Italy, Bulgaria, Turkey, Arabia and Persia are in the area destined to be covered before

[7] See pages 57-8 herein.

long by a new ocean, dotted by a few islands that once were mountain peaks. . . . When this internal heat has blown a big abscess under the cold surface of the earth, the top crust will crack, as it has done on a titanic scale three times in the past 5,000 years. . . . And the mapmakers will need to get busy redesigning their charts. . . . To-day the ancient volcanic areas of Italy, Eastern Europe and Western Asia and Iceland are ready for that final disruptive action which will remove fully one-third of the present earth areas and submerge their remnants beneath the waters of the Atlantic, the North Sea, the Ægean, the Indian Ocean and the Pacific. But not only will a new continent appear from Australia and the Pacific depth, but there will be a *change of polar axes,* formed of regions now in more temperate climes. . . . There seems to be a periodicity in such cataclysms, whose details are but faintly established, beginning historically with the Biblical deluge about 2316 B.C. Etna and Stromboli have been active since long before the Christian era. Hecklafer even longer. Such activity means that constant eating away by internal fires of the overhead walls is going on. When will these walls be so weakened that the crevassing occurs? It would be a foolish guess to estimate it in years though the earth seems ripe."[8]

[8] *United News,* June 20, 1923. "Towns destroyed by quake and fire; many isles rocked. Crete and Rhodes are badly shaken. Vast damage in region of the Mediterranean and Aegean Seas. Egypt, Ionians and many other places suffer loss; people in consternation. Five shocks were recorded in 48 hours." *Washington Post,* June 28, 1926.

The continental changes referred to above sometimes require thousands of years for the great cycle of their complete readjustment, but at every sub-cycle minor changes occur which, while relatively local, nevertheless are cataclysmic to the people inhabiting the affected regions. Just now the Earth, having entered upon the new Aquarian Age or cycle, has reached a point in its evolution when such minor cataclysms are due to begin, and in fact have already begun. That our present day is such a period of culmination *is recognized by all groups of students* who have given any special study to the subject, and although they often arrive at their conclusions from widely different standpoints and from different data, they are *practically unanimous as to the time and the general regions* most likely to be affected.

All of which is evidence that the change of Earth conditions has already begun, and as it progresses there must naturally be a shifting of the great oceans, certain countries becoming submerged and others raised up, as indicated in our *Prophecy of the King of the World.*

The coming changes may not involve the destruction of an entire continent and a whole Race, as in the days of Lemuria and Atlantis, but they will, nevertheless, be vast in extent, and it seems to be the consensus of opinion that they will be largely centered in Europe and the Near East and along the Western coast of America, although with marked reverberations in more distant regions.

CHAPTER III

THE PHILOSOPHY OF PLANETARY CHANGES

"Esoteric Science teaches that every sound in the visible world awakens its corresponding sound in the invisible realms, and arouses to action some force or other on the occult side of Nature." *The Secret Doctrine,* Blavatsky, iii, 451.

"This know also, that in the last days perilous times shall come. For men shall be lovers of their own selves, covetous, boasters, proud, blasphemers, disobedient to parents, unthankful, unholy . . . despisers of those that are good . . . lovers of pleasures more than lovers of God; having a form of holiness, but denying the power thereof." *II Timothy,* i, 5.

"I will pray with the Spirit, and I will pray with understanding also." *I Corinthians,* xiv, 15.

In the previous chapter we have pointed out that changes in the surface of the globe are normal, periodic, cyclic and inevitable, owing to the necessary rearrangement of the land and water areas as the axis of the Earth slowly swings from the perpendicular to the horizontal and back again in its cyclic arc of revolution.

"Esoteric Philosophy . . . teaches distinctly, that after the first geological disturbance of the Earth's axis, which ended in the sweeping down to the bottom of the seas the whole of the Second Continent, with its primeval races—of which successive Continents or 'Earths' Atlantis was the fourth—there came another disturbance owing to the axis again resuming its previous degree of inclination as rapidly as it had changed it; when the Earth was indeed once more *raised* out of the waters. . . . There have already been four such axial disturbances. The old Continents—save the first—were sucked in by the oceans, other lands appeared. . . . The face of the Globe was completely changed each time; the 'survival of the fittest' nations and races was secured *through timely help;* and the unfit ones—the failures—were disposed of by being swept off the face of the Earth."[1]

These great continental cataclysms are related to Major or Root Races and the Sidereal Year of nearly 26,000 years.

"Every Sidereal Year the tropics recede four degrees in each revolution from the equinoctial points, as the equator turns through the zodiacal constellations. . . . It has still two and a half degrees to run before the end of the Sidereal Year. This gives humanity in general, and our civilized races in particular, a reprieve of about 16,000 years."[2]

Therefore it is not a general continental cataclysm that is facing humanity at this time, but a relatively minor although extensive one. For "The sub-races are also subject to the same cleansing process, and the side branchlets or family-races as well."[2] And it is the changes due at the winding up of such a sub-race—the fifth—that are at hand to-day.

To students who are not familiar with the Cosmic Philosophy of *The Order of Christian Mystics* and who

[1] *The Secret Doctrine*, Blavatsky, ii, 344.
[2] *Ibid.*, ii, 345, 344

are not accustomed to a planetary viewpoint, instead of a local and therefore very limited one, it may seem fantastic to assert that the thoughts and actions of humanity have anything to do with storms, earthquakes and cataclysms. But a deeper study of the Law of Cause and Effect called Karma, and of the radio-activity of living forces will show that this is so.

The forces of Nature operate in a rhythmic and cyclic manner, season following season with the precision of a gigantic cosmic clock. These changes normally come about in a harmonious manner. The snow falls gently to blanket the Earth, protect the seeds from winter-killing by the intense cold, and to fill Nature's reservoirs with moisture for the coming season; the rain descends to refresh the Earth and its children and supply them with water; the wind blows mildly or strongly to circulate and purify the atmosphere according to the meteorological conditions, all in peace and harmony and coöperation. But where great clouds of inharmonious mental and magnetic force have been generated by mankind they tend to find expression through the forces of Nature, and thus the equilibrium and rhythmic harmony of Nature is upset and destructive expressions of normally constructive Nature-forces take place.

"Let us keep in mind that the heresies of Galileo's day are now universally accepted scientific facts."

If the seemingly absurd theory that such vastly remote causes as storms in the photosphere of the Sun (sun-spots) can so upset the magnetic balance of the Earth and its atmosphere as to produce marked climatic changes has been proved true and accepted as scientifically correct; if the invisible radiations of human thought exert a sufficiently physical force to affect a photographic plate and produce a skotograph [8] of the thought held at the time, as in the hundreds of experiments of Dr. Baraduc in Paris, is it any more strange or unreasonable to assert that an accumulation of millions of such streams of thought-force of an intensely inharmonious character should affect and upset the harmonious balance of Nature-forces and find expression in destructive storms? For it is thus that Nature becomes an agent for the execution of karmic law which brings to mankind the results of the forces it has generated. All religions and philosophies teach, as a fundamental law, that "whatsoever a man soweth, that shall he reap," both individually and collectively, and usually through such apparently natural events as those of Nature.

The law of the radio-active nature of thought and the power of its broadcasting to produce physical results was well known to the ancients and *is especially taught* in many places in the *Bible*. For instance, *Jeremiah* (vi, 19) tells us: "Hear, O earth: behold, I will bring evil upon this people, *even the fruits of their thoughts*, because they have not harkened unto my words, nor my law, but rejected it." Again, speaking of blessings expected, he tells us (v, 25) that, "Your iniquities have turned away these things, and your sins have withholden good things from you." "Curse not the king, no not in thy thought . . . for a bird of

[8] A picture taken without the use of light of any kind.

the air shall carry the voice, and that which hath wings shall tell the matter." [4]

"An Occultist or a Philosopher will not speak of the goodness or cruelty of Providence; but . . . he will nevertheless teach that it guards the good and watches over them in this and future lives; and that it punishes the evil-doer . . . so long, indeed, as the effect of his having thrown into perturbation even the smallest atom in the infinite World of Harmony has not been finally adjusted. For the only decree of Karma—an eternal and immutable decree—is absolute Harmony in the world of Matter as it is in the world of Spirit. *It is not, therefore, Karma that rewards or punishes,* but it is *we who reward or punish ourselves*, according as we work with, through and along with Nature, abiding by the laws on which harmony depends, or—breaking them." [5]

As we have said elsewhere: "When storms, earthquakes, tidal waves, volcanic outbursts or catastrophes of other kinds take place many say, 'Behold the work of God! How insignificant is man!' This is false. God never made a storm or a catastrophe of any kind, for God is the great Law of Love. They are all evidences of man's power. Had man never sent out evil thoughts, wicked words, blasphemies and curses, the Earth's aura could never be so charged with destructive forces that a catastrophe was necessary to dissipate them and bring about equilibrium. . . . 'Thus saith the Lord of hosts, Behold, evil shall go forth from

[4] *Ecclesiastes,* x, 20.
[5] *The Secret Doctrine,* Blavatsky, i, 704-5.

nation to nation, and a great whirlwind shall be raised up from the coasts of the earth.'[6] . . . Although the tornado is a result of the inharmony and impurity created by man, still it is used as an agent of Karma to dissipate the accumulated forces of evil and to readjust the atmosphere and permit new conditions more advantageous for the evolution of the planet and its inhabitants to manifest. The tornado was not the *cause* of the destruction of life and property in its path, it was merely the *agent* for adjusting the causes *set up by man*. . . . The fundamental idea of Karma is Harmony. It is not a punishment; not even an inevitable law of suffering which you must endure . . . not one of punishment for past failures, but that you may learn your lessons and gain as quickly as possible the Soul qualities needed, that you may fulfill your destiny, your special place and work in the Grand Plan." [7]

With this brief survey of the cyclic law of geological changes in mind, the point we wish to emphasize is that while such geological changes are due to take place *it rests with humanity how these changes shall come about*, gradually and harmoniously or suddenly and cataclysmically. As the one called the King of the World[8] told us in a talk some months ago: [9]

"The time is coming *shortly* when there must be wonderful changes take place in the Earth. These changes can be made in peace and quietness, but *man forbids*. We wait for the New Day to come, and the

[6] *Jeremiah*, xxv, 32.
[7] *The Voice of Isis*, Curtiss, 172, 116-7.
[8] See Chapter IV herein.
[9] July 2, 1925.

great tiger who is my footstool, who sleeps beneath my feet, crawls out and gives his cries. And when these cries are heard by the children of men fear quickens in their hearts and their blood runs cold like ice-water, and they run to and fro crying out for the mountains to fall upon them as the mighty changes take place. But the All-Powerful One never meant it to be thus.

"The changes we must have, but they should come like the changes between day and night; like the coming of the gentle dawn as the stars one by one withdraw their light as they draw back the curtains of the night and say a beautiful and smiling adieu to the Earth. And those who are watching the tides of the ocean hear them lap soft sentences and whisper murmuringly in the ear gentle blessings for what the night has brought forth. Then the Sun comes up out of the ocean where it has hidden its face and looks upon his handiwork. This is the way the changes should come.

"This is the Law of God Almighty. The All-Powerful One has willed it so, and all creation should go on in rhythmic harmony and beauty, one day after another as the mystery of understanding is brought forth. But, alas, humanity's consciousness has stopped this; for it cannot understand the words and sounds. The tones of their words may fly up to the throne of the Eternal Ever-Living One, but their hearts, which gave utterance to them, are like locked doors.

"O ye men of Earth! O ye women of Earth! Why are ye like dumb driven cattle, seeking for your sustenance by ravening one another? baying at the moon; huddling together in the darkness of the night; seeking in the caverns and crevices of the Earth for treasure, only physical treasure! The only treasure that God, the Almighty Ever-Lasting One, has given to man is the treasure of His words. Can ye wonder then if the changes from one great Cosmic Day to another come like crashes? come like the dissolution of the foundations of the Earth?"

It should be remembered that recent investigations into the radio-active power of mental forces teaches us that the magnetic currents which sustain the crust of the Earth can be so upset and made to fluctuate by the powerful though subtile vibrations generated by mankind that the vast structural changes which are inevitable are precipitated cataclysmically. On the other hand, harmonious vibrations generated by humanity through love, brotherhood, coöperation and the definite currents of constructive cosmic energy which can be invoked through prayer and aspiration—as testified to by all religions in all ages—tend to neutralize the inharmonious and destructive vibrations and sustain the normal Earth-currents. While the natural and cyclic changes in the Earth's surface do not come as punishment for man's sins—for our God is a God of Love and mercy—yet the radio-active power of man's evil and destructive vibrations can so unbalance conditions that they precipitate normal changes in a cataclysmic manner.

In addition to this we know that we have already entered the great cycle during which the axis of the Earth is slowly returning to its former horizontal position, preparatory to the closing or Golden Age of this World

Period or Manvantara, when perpetual summer will again reign as it did in the opening Golden Age of humanity. Although this final result will not be reached until the time of the Seventh Great Race [10] thousands of years hence, nevertheless the process has already definitely begun and the changes will be sufficiently rapid to give the sixth sub-race of the present Aryan Race its (a minor) Golden Age. But the changes foreshadowed in the *Prophecies* may well be close at hand, much sooner in years than many imagine.

Naturally, those who do not correlate with the new spiritual keynote now set for the coming sixth sub-race will tend to go on from one excess to another—as seen in the present jazz age—and from one disbelief to another; disbelief in God and in spiritual Beings and forces; disbelief in religion, in law, in medicine, in coöperation, in unselfishness and in Good, in fact in everything but selfishness, self-indulgence and physical force.

All those who refuse to set a higher spiritual standard and vibration for their thoughts, their lives and their conduct, together with those whose Karma is such that *it would not be just or kind* of the Great Law to expect them to make so great an advance in so short a time, will naturally be removed so that the more spiritually advanced ones who are left will be in sufficient majority to dictate the principles and ideals under which the surviving mankind shall exist and be gov-

[10] For details see *The Voice of Isis,* Curtiss, 239, *The Message of Aquaria,* Curtiss, 41, 126.

erned, unhampered by the ridicule and opposition of those who cannot comprehend such ideals, instead of allowing the decisions to be made by those ignorant of fundamental spiritual principles or those who refuse to follow them because their minds are inflamed by selfishness, greed, hatred and revenge. Real world progress cannot be made until the best good of humanity as a whole is the basic consideration of conferences among nations.

Just as there are two great currents of force winding around the spinal column and crossing over at certain centers in man—as symbolized by the serpents of the Caduceus—so there are corresponding magnetic currents slowly traversing the Earth from pole to pole and with corresponding crossings at certain cycles. As these crossings take place they cannot fail to bring about great changes, unsuspected and little understood conditions, both in man and the planet. One of the reasons why we are expecting such radical changes is because the Earth is now approaching such a crossing over of great planetary currents. For in the history of the Earth these periods have always been marked by terrific changes involving earthquakes, intense volcanic outbursts, unseasonable weather, with intense heat and bitter cold, and many other unusual conditions. These will seem more widespread than in former times because of our more universal means of communication.

These periods have also been marked by a great dominance of mind over Spirit and a stamping out almost entirely of all that represents the Divine Mother side of life, the spirit of Divine Love and Compassion. And just as with the individual who puts his whole attention upon the development of mind and uses the powers thus gained to achieve personal aggrandizement and power to dominate others, the result must be a fall and death and a temporary forgetting of all that has been accomplished, so is it with nations and peoples. If in the past the ambition of one great nation to dominate the commerce, wealth and the power of the world could bring on the last World War, so to-day the ambition of a certain nation to seize and dismember other nations, as a step toward dominating the Mediterranean Sea, may well precipitate conditions which will consolidate the peoples of Asia against Europe and so lead to the fifth great Asiatic invasion[11] so frequently prophesied, as recounted on pages 20-23, 56-57.

Such another World War might well be sufficient to unbalance the Earth-currents, already still fluctuating from the effects of the last Great War, and precipitate the catastrophes in Europe and the Near East. For the same forces which were the instruments through which the catastrophes at the last crossing over were brought about ages ago are now about to complete another turn around the globe and another crossing over. And if such a crossing over is not accomplished normally: if it is perturbed by the destructive vibrations of intense antagonism and hatred of whole nations, of injustice, bloodshed and all the horrors of another World War, it may well result in disasters

[11] Previous invasions: the Huns in 451 A.D.; the Arabs in 732 A.D.; the Mongols in 1241 A.D.; the Turks in 1683 A.D.

which will wipe out whole nations and necessitate a reconstruction of civilization by those that are left.

In a certain sense these two great Earth-currents act as the currents of past and future Karma; the Karma of ancient Lemuria which is now slowly rising in the Pacific and must needs meet and conquer the Karma which sunk it. While that great continent has remained beneath the waters undergoing its physical cleansing, its peoples have been incarnating in later Races and learning great lessons, yet every one now in incarnation who was associated with the fall of Lemuria will be more or less affected by the coming changes. The Great Law which has been their guide throughout succeeding ages and which has sustained them in their effort to redeem their Karma, will still guide and sustain them *wherever it is best for them to be.* For not one who has striven sincerely to face and work out that old Karma and advance spiritually and help make the world better for all mankind but will be taken care of *wherever their inner guidance impels them to live.* Therefore "Fear ye not, stand still and see the salvation of the Lord, which he will shew you to-day."

Some few students who do not sufficiently understand our philosophy have written that the sweeping away of thousands or millions in the coming storms, plagues, disasters and cataclysms, was a terrible and horrible idea to contemplate, although over ten million were killed in the late World War and over fifty-two millions more died from its after-effects—famines, plagues, etc., with 140,000,000 injured, a total of more than 10 per cent. of the world's population! [12] But even if the *Prophecies* were fulfilled in a day, those thus removed from physical manifestation would only be reaping the results of the causes they *as nations and peoples* had set up. And even this scientifically just retribution would not be an evidence that they had been deserted and condemned by the God of Divine Love and Wisdom—which is also Justice—but rather had been removed to make them *cease generating further results of that kind,* and to give them an opportunity to see the unhappy results which their wrong standards of thought and action had brought about, and to learn their needed lessons and prepare them for more positive spiritual advance in subsequent incarnations.

Those who refuse to heed the warnings and suffer now were among those who helped to generate the causes of inharmony which made the Earth changes focalize in their particular region and involve them, even though they were apparently innocent in this life. Far from this being a time to "eat, drink and be merry, for to-morrow we die" it is a time for prayer and meditation; for the radiation of definite spiritual forces; for a spiritual and moral housecleaning for both individuals and nations if the disasters are to be minimized.

Our readers, however, should have no fear of these catastrophes, for we have explained *why* and *how* these seeming disasters are but an outworking of the Great Law, and that since *there is no death to the Soul,* the sweeping out of incarnation of even millions of Souls

[12] *Report of the League of Red Cross Societies,* June, 1926.

may be for their greatest good and in the greatest love, for such a removal from Earth-life would give them an opportunity to learn greater lessons and make greater progress before their next incarnation than the longest possible life on Earth, especially in its present upset condition, could bring about. Such catastrophes would also bring about a great development of love, sympathy, brotherhood and coöperation in those who were left behind.

CHAPTER IV

THE KING OF THE WORLD

"And though the Lord give you the bread of adversity, and the water of affliction, yet shall not thy teachers be removed into a corner any more, but thine eyes shall see thy teachers. And thine ears shall hear a word behind thee, saying, This is the way, walk ye in it." *Isaiah,* xxx, 20-1.

"Press on, my warriors, fear not the fray!
We are the Conquerors; our Voice obey.
Sound loud the trumpet blast, happy and free,
Tell of the Day Star that is destined to be."
Harriette Augusta Curtiss in *Realms of the Living Dead,* 176.

In his remarkable book, *Beasts, Men and Gods,* published in 1922, Dr. Ferdinand Ossendowski, formerly Professor of Chemistry and Economical Geography in the Polytechnic Institut of Petrograd, and later Professor of Chemistry at the Polish University at Warsaw, reports a prophecy, given as far back as 1890, to the Hutuktu (Abbott) of the Narabanchi Monastery in Mongolia by the Great Unknown who, throughout Asia, is called the King of the World. This prophecy described the conditions that were coming to humanity during the following fifty years (1890-1940)—much of which was literally fulfilled during the World War of 1914-18—as follows:

"More and more people will forget their souls and care about their bodies. The greatest sin and corruption will reign on earth. . . . The crowns of kings, great and small, will fall . . . one, two, three, four, five, six, seven, eight. . . . There will be a terrible battle among all peoples. (The World War.) The seas will become red . . . the earth and the bottom of the sea will be strewn with bones . . . kingdoms will be scattered . . . whole peoples will die . . . hunger, disease, crimes unknown to law, never before seen in the world . . . the ancient roads will be covered with crowds wandering from one place to another. . . . All the earth will be emptied. God will turn away from it and over it there will be only night and death. Then I shall send a people, now unknown, which shall tear out the weeds of madness and vice with a strong hand, and I will lead those who still remain faithful to the spirit of man in the fight against Evil. They will found a new life on the earth purified by the death of nations. . . . The King of the World will appear before all people when the time shall have arrived for him to lead all the good people of the world against all the bad; but this time has not yet come. The most evil among mankind have not yet been born."[1]

In an article in *The Century Magazine* for December, 1923,[2] Professor Ossendowski states that among various Asiatic peoples there exists, "a watchword proclaiming the superiority of the spiritual strength of the East, and affirming the necessity of forcing all humanity to accept its will and its world-outlook, even

[1] *Beasts, Men and Gods,* Ossendowski, 312-13-14.
[2] Pages 247, 256.

at the cost of general blood-spilling, even by hurling Asiatic multitudes upon the nations rotting in the bog of European civilization.

"Accordingly, at the fires of the nomad shepherds of the prairies, in the Tzaidam marshes in northern Thibet, in the Himalayas, on the banks of the Hind and the Ganges, in Asia Minor, in Iran, in the valleys of the Yang-tse and the Hwang-po, people of different colors, tribes, races and creeds, but united by the common bond of Asiatic ideology, talk, discuss, sing, and dream about the approaching hour, when the hand of the Asiatic will be the hand of karma and will execute the decrees of fate . . . to an attack against the white race—an attack which is the dream of some Asiatic circles. . . . At all events, it is more than probable that the white race will be obliged to reckon with the influence of the now only legendary King of the World."

The latter part of the above prophecy seems to corroborate the prophecy of Mr. Cromer regarding an Asiatic invasion as given on page 23.

During her remarkable visit to Lhasa, the capital of Thibet, Mme. Alexandria David-Neel relates that: "Hatred of Europeans is sown in many remote corners of Asia. Many partisans stand ready to support the expected warrior Messiah, who, according to the prophets, will arise before long in the northern land, unite all Asia under his victorious sword and cast out the impure, demoniacal Westerners." [8]

[8] *Asia Magazine,* July, 1926, 627.

Already the Japanese have called a Pan-Asiatic Union Conference to meet at Nagasaki on August 1st, 1926, "designed to bind the nations of the Orient in the same sort of fashion as the Pan-American Union links the nations of the Western Hemisphere. . . . There is unfortunately an ominous ring in the title of the Pan-Asiatic Society. There is considerable justification for the apprehensions, but not, as yet, for the accompanying fears. . . . The unity and peace of Asia . . . are the objectives . . . of the leaders who hope, sooner or later, to bring about a serious 'Asia for the Asiatics' situation." [4]

In our lesson for December, 1922, we gave out a prophecy given to *The Order of Christian Mystics* by this same mysterious King of the World which read as follows:

"I see a great and devastating Flame sweeping the world from East to West; a Flame of fire; a Flame of sword and famine and murder and bitterness and death. I see the peoples of the Earth, each one with its hand lifted against its brother; each country seeking for its own; men dying, dying and cursing God with every dying breath, and sowing the seed of new and more frightful Flames.

"I see descending from on high the mighty Angel with the Flaming Sword; for only fire can purify hate. I see this Flame of Purification sweeping the Earth from East to West, from the rising of the Sun to the going down of the Sun.

[4] *Washington Star,* March 14, 1926.

"Five countries are left. The rest sink beneath the seas. Five countries! Five lands like fingers on a man's hand! Four shall be great and one small, but out of the smallest there grows the greatest Light. Then comes redemption. Then comes that which alone can make this world to be reborn, once more human, like a babe laid in a manger, cradled in its mother's arms.

"I see a great mountain lifted up in the midst of the countries which are left, and from its top there radiates the Light of the Spiritual Sun. And I see the remnants of mankind bathed in its Radiance.

"Think not that any country in this broad world can escape. The Flame sweeps onward and over. Only those who have the Flame of the Living Christ in their hearts shall survive.

"I speak, for this is my world. Into my hands it has been given. I stretch out my hand and each finger represents a point of force, a place where the great living Power of the Sun has breathed into it the life (fire) which is immortal.

"Where are my children? They are dying. They are being murdered and starved. They are being scattered like sheep on the cold bare mountain tops, homeless and friendless. For a time I bow to the inevitable. I wait. I wait that a Greater than I may read you the riddle of this Dark Star." [5]

[5] The vision that came with the prophecy was that of an immense hand with the wrist to the North, the thumb to the East, the little finger to the extreme West and all the fingers widely spread. On the little finger a light seemed to be glowing under ashes. This light slowly spread and grew brighter until finally a hill rose up in

It was at first thought that the King of the World was the Planetary Ruler of the Earth, but later instruction from the King himself explained that he was a great Atlantean Master who had passed through the process of physical regeneration and so was able to retain and renew his physical body indefinitely. During the ensuing ages he had developed greater and greater powers and had been entrusted with greater and greater tasks until he became the chief representative on Earth of the celestial Ruler of our globe.

Since the publication of this *Prophecy*, in December, 1922, we have had many inquiries for further details as to this *Prophecy*, but few further details can be given. Remember that the *Prophecy* did not come from the Teacher of *The Order of Christian Mystics* nor from the Coming Avatar, but from the representative of the Planetary Ruler of this globe, the Earth, and those few who heard it were too greatly awed to ask for details during that brief visit. The only detail that we can give is that the country represented by "the little finger" was not Japan, as some supposed, but probably some part of Western North America. The special region cannot be indicated until after the rising of Lemuria and the settling and readjustment of the continent.

To us the *Prophecy* indicated that which will come to pass *if humanity persists in its present course* and

the middle of the back of the hand and when the light from the little finger reached it it broke out into a radiant shining which covered the whole Earth. No limit as to time was given in this prophecy, both the time and the degree of the changes depending largely upon the character of the forces engendered by humanity.

continues to send out destructive vibrations of inharmony, antagonism, hatred, selfishness and greed, instead of the constructive vibrations of brotherhood and coöperation. That the latter are the most vital needs of the world to-day is corroborated by United States Senators, officials and prominent business men after returning from Europe, who practically agree with Senator McCormick of Illinois, who is quoted as saying that: "More important to the rehabilitation of Europe than any Conference, than any agreement between statesmen and financiers can be, is *the exorcism of the spirit of hate and greed* which animates governments and peoples. Unless the peoples are moved by a Christian *will to peace* and by a Christian comity, there can be no real peace in Europe."

While the Earth-children are scattered through all countries they are most concentrated in the Far East. They are concentrated in Asia because there they are less mingled with children of other planets, and hence are able to correlate more readily with the consciousness of the Earth and come more fully under the guidance of their King, where in certain sacred monasteries He has appeared and given personal instruction. They must be judged as good or bad, not according to western standards, but according to their obedience or disobedience to the principles of their religion.

By Earth-children we do not mean those who in this incarnation are born astrologically under the earth signs, for we must all incarnate many times under all the astrological signs ere Mastery is attained. The Earth-children are those who came to this planet primarily because, through affinity, it was their natural habitat. These Souls naturally owe allegiance and worship to their divine Progenitor, hence we find them following almost exclusively the forms of worship and religion, ethics and morals inspired by that Progenitor.

At the same time we know that there are millions of Souls on Earth who come from all the other planets of this system and some from other systems, attracted to this newest field of experience, some few advanced Souls volunteering to come to act as helpers and teachers of mankind, but the majority to gain the new and much needed experience of Earth conditions. Try to picture to yourself this great truth. See the little planet Earth newly born, born from the accumulated star dust and meteors, from the left-overs cast off from other greater and mightier systems, passing through its fiery birth, and within its bosom holding fast the germs of living powers, each destined to play its part in the great drama which is now being staged thereon. Some may be born of the very Earth itself and with the essence of the Earth Spirit breathed into them, others may have traveled eons of ages through time and space from far-distant planets or systems. They may have voluntarily chosen and consciously given up their Soul-home and their realization of the great planetry Being who is their Father that they might come to help on the evolution of this new and infant world, nevertheless the instant they enter the Earth's aura and commingle in its forces they become clothed in Earth materials and this Earth covering blinds them into forgetfulness of that which they have left behind.

In view of the above we can now understand why the destructive aspect of the Flame of Purification will spread from the East to the West and will ultimately sweep all nations, each suffering according to the amount of inharmony, unbrotherliness, antagonism, and evil there is to be consumed. We can correlate with the Flame and make the fire our servant only as we strive to become one with the Divine Fire of the Living Christ and willingly allow it to burn from us all inharmony and impurity, all that holds back the manifestation of our Real or Divine Self.

Once we have grasped the idea that the Flame consumes only that which is evil or which must be transmuted to make room for the Divine Life and Joy of those who fearlessly face self and bravely strive to conquer all that is not in harmony with the Law, then, like Shadrach, Meshach and Abednego, even though we seem bound hand and foot and thrown into the midst of the fiery furnace—the flames of purgation now sweeping the Earth—when the morning of the New Day dawns we will be found walking free in the midst of the Flame because the Lord Christ walks with us.

CHAPTER V

THE HEART OF THE WORLD

"Occult Philosophy teaches that even now, under our very eyes, the new Race and races are preparing to be formed, and that it is in America that the transformation will take place, and has already silently commenced." *The Secret Doctrine*, Blavatsky, ii, 463.

"To do justice and judgment is more acceptable to the Lord than sacrifice." *Proverbs*, xxi, 3.

The Cosmic Philosophy of *The Order of Christian Mystics* teaches that the cycle of human evolution—from the primitive to perfection—extends throughout seven Major or Root Races, one succeeding the other through immense periods of time and each overlapping the other for many ages.[1] Each Major Race has seven sub-races, each of which is composed of many nations and peoples. Each sub-race spreads over and occupies a particular area, sometimes even a continent, almost exclusively. As each sub-race grows in power, since it is the youngest and most virile, its nations gradually become the leaders for its cycle.

It is generally accepted that America is to be the seat of the coming new sub-race, the sixth sub-race of the fifth Major or Aryan Race.

"Pure Anglo-Saxons hardly three hundred years ago, the Americans of the United States have already be-

[1] For details see *The Voice of Isis*, Curtiss, Chapt. xvii.

come a nation apart, and owing to a strong admixture of various nationalities, almost a race *sui generis,* not only mentally, but also physically. Thus Americans have become in only three centuries a 'primary race,' temporarily, before becoming a race apart, and strongly separated from other now existing races. They are, in short, the germs of the *sixth* sub-race, and in some few hundred years more, will become most decidedly the pioneers of the Race which must succeed to the present European or fifth sub-race, in all its new characteristics." [2]

Some teachers have given out that California is to be the seat of a new Race, without making it plain that it is only a sub-race to which they refer and not a Major Race. But since even a sub-race extends through more than 210,000 years [3] and its component family races more than 30,000 years each, it will be at least 10,000 before even a new family race reaches the zenith of its power and development. And thousands of years before it reaches that point of its development—even within a comparatively few years—the changes incident to the reëmergence of the great continent of Lemuria from the waters of the Pacific will so modify California that it will hardly be recognizable. What remains of its present coast cities will be left far inland and separated from the sea by great stretches of newly risen land which will be uninhabitable for ages while it is undergoing its period of preparation.

[2] *The Secret Doctrine,* Blavatsky, ii, 463-4.
[3] For details see *The Message of Aquaria,* Curtiss, 42.

For when a continent sinks beneath the sea it undergoes a cleansing and purifying process to fit it for rehabitation by those who, through many incarnations during the ages of its submersion, have so progressed that they require new and purified conditions ere they can incarnate on their home-land when it again emerges from the sea. The law is that at certain stages of evolution both continents and humanity must be purified first by water and then by fire. In the human being the personality is first cleansed by the salt tears of suffering and then by the fire of experience. In the case of a continent it is first purified by the salt water,[4] then it rises to lie as a desolate desert waste for ages while the volcanic fires and the baking action of the sun purify it as by fire, much as flour is first mixed with water and then baked in the oven ere it is fit for food.

While children who are the forerunners and pioneers of the new sub-race are being born in California, they are also being born in the Eastern states in even greater numbers, because more densely populated. Therefore it will be many generations ere California will be especially distinguished in that respect. It is not California especially that must be prepared to receive the sensitive and advanced Souls of the new sub-race, but the entire country.

It is a part of the cosmic scheme or Divine Plan that America, as it develops and proves itself, is destined to become the leading nation of the new Aquarian Age into which the world has recently entered. America is

[4] For details see *The Voice of Isis,* Curtiss, Chapt. xxxi.

already called the most advanced nation in the world. As far as achievements of mind, of new inventions, of mechanical and material development and in wealth and luxury she already leads the world. But in addition to her material achievements she has proved herself the most capable of using the products of the world for the highest ends, for she has unselfishly spent hundreds of millions of dollars and has gone to the ends of the Earth to feed and clothe and bring help to foreign cities, nations and peoples in distress, whether suffering from disasters, famines, plagues or the impoverishing results of war.

But in spite of all her generosity and unselfishness she has much Karma to reap, a great expansion of consciousness to undergo and a great realization of injustice done and its correction to bring about ere she can become the moral as well as the material leader of the world. Much of the injustice done to the negro during the days of slavery has been corrected by making him a citizen and free to exercise all the privileges of a citizen, not only to vote but to live where he pleases, to go and come without restraint and to work out his destiny according to his racial capacity, which citizenship privileges are denied to the Indian.

According to a message recently received from the Master: "There are many things from which this nation must be cleansed, and her day of purgation is drawing nigh. Oh, if I could only say: 'This is my country. These are my chosen people, for I have chosen them that they shall prevail and rule the world!' How easy and satisfactory such a statement would be! But it is not so. America, with all her possessions, her vast lands, her great wealth, her so-called advanced civilization, nevertheless must have her time of reckoning, her time of housecleaning.

"There is one special blot upon the escutcheon of this nation, and until it is recognized and something is done to bring about justice and an understanding and better conditions, there will be little hope of this country escaping the terrible cataclysms that are to come. I speak of its treatment of the original lords of this great land, the real Americans, now called the Indians. Ever since the sinking of Atlantis, when some of the Wise Men of that country took refuge on what is now known as America, their descendants have occupied the land. When, after ages and ages, the white man came he made no attempt to understand them, but called them ignorant savages and heathen. Then came his war of extermination, which failed to exterminate; a war of stupidity and ignorance, a wilful and persistent ignoring that the Indian had any rights, any religion, any ideals worthy of recognition or consideration. . . .

"As to their religion, of course the wonderful religion taught by the better class of Atlanteans of the Right Hand Path gradually degenerated through the ages, yet some of the Indians still retain many mysterious gifts and practices which are remnants of the Atlantean Mysteries, but which were unrecognized by the ignorant white people who seized their possessions without compensation and tried to push the Indians off the Earth. . . . Those who are their priests, those who have passed the initiations—initiations so intense and searching that they bring out the most heroic powers of body and soul—have many marvelous powers and attainments. . . . No ordinary people could live and maintain their own life, their nationality and their religion in the United States unless they had powers little dreamed of by the white man. Indeed, the white man is responsible for the suppression and killing out, in the younger generation of Indians, of *even the memory* of their ancient mysteries, many of their Wise Men having voluntarily withdrawn from Earth life. . . .

"Until this great wrong has been righted; until America begins to recognize and learn the mysteries, both as to religion, the development of the mystic centers in the body, and many wonderful ways of living which the Indian could teach her, and is willing to receive and learn them from him as from a brother, she will never reach the heights of her glory."

Not only was great injustice done the Indians in the past, but it still continues to be done to-day. Although technically granted citizenship they are not permitted to enjoy or exercise its privileges, not even allowed to seek redress in court—for tribal affairs—as is freely granted the negro, without the special permission of Congress. Also, our Government, after persuading the Indians to enter various treaties with it, has itself violated nearly every one of them, and the Indians are without redress in court. These are not matters of opinion, but are facts of public record.[5] Could there be any greater injustice and denial of rights to United States citizens in direct violation of the Constitution? No wonder we are told that such a constant and still continuing injustice must have a marked effect upon the Karma of the whole nation until it is redeemed.

The point is that even though the Indian did little to cultivate the soil and occupy the land in an agricultural sense, he should have been properly compensated for being driven from his forest and prairie hunting grounds into the arid desert regions which no one else wanted until coal and oil were found upon them. The least America can do is to fulfill the solemn obligations voluntarily assumed by her in her many treaties with the Indians.

"The leaders of this nation should remember that the Indians are not an unintelligent and inferior race, but are remnants of the once mightiest of Races which reached the highest pinnacle of mental attainment and magical powers before the sinking of their continent (Atlantis). You talk about the mysteries of Egypt and the Far East! They are as nothing when compared to some of the mysteries known to and kept alive through practice by certain Indian priests. . . . You should do all you can to induce Congress to right the injustice, but you should also pray and invoke the higher powers to help you save America from such a Karma. Let America look to the power of her vital inner strength; not the strength of arms or of great

[5] For particulars send a stamp to the *National Council of American Indians*, Transportation Building, Washington, D. C.

wealth, but the strength of justice, of Karma redeemed, the strength of the Man Who Knows. There is hope if there are even a few determined ones who can believe in their fellow men, who can realize that money is not all, that head-learning is not all; for it is only trained and developed mind wedded to awakened heart that can carry you through the Day of Reckoning that is now dawning. Let all who will raise their hands to heaven morning, noon and night and cry aloud:

> Justice for the Indian!
> A clean escutcheon for our country!
> The shortening of the Days of Tribulation! *

"We are now entering upon a great age of testing. America is a wonderful country and should be the Heart of the World, but to be chosen and have the opportunity does not mean that she has attained that position already. With all her great attainments, her vast wealth, her mighty territory, her great abilities, she could hold the world in her grasp. America emerged from the World War as a great world power, and had she then taken her rightful place at the head

* Within one month after our students throughout the world began repeating the prayer for *Justice for the Indian* the infamous oil leasing bill was defeated. This bill would have deprived the Indians of their title to their unallotted lands and imposed a 37½ per cent income tax! The Senate has now passed a bill drafted by the friends of the Indians permanently safeguarding their ownership of their lands, and there is every prospect of their being allowed to exercise the full privileges of the citizenship conferred upon them in 1924. No such sweeping defeat of the autocratic Indian Bureau has ever taken place in Indian history. So let us keep up the prayer and let the good work go on to completion.—*The Authors.*

of the League of Nations, as was her destiny, she could easily have led the world. But now it is too late. Since her repudiation of her great mission and her great opportunity she lost her moral leadership and it will be wise for her to keep free from European entanglements until she is able to dominate other than by her arms or her wealth. This she will not be able to do until she corrects injustice and disregard for law at home, and begins to recognize and utilize some of the mysterious higher and super-physical powers already known to the Indians. . . .

"This great nation is the hope of the Living Power that is to precede the manifestation of the beloved Son of God, but how can such a manifestation take place where all is dominated by materiality, by business strife and political turmoil?

"Whenever the Earth is to pass through a great cataclysm and pass through a time of necessary purification, some positive manifestation of the great Avatar destined to come as the Savior of mankind is given to humanity and is noted by its seers, prophets and awakened ones. Such a manifestation of the loving Son of God has already been shown to you and its significance pointed out. Hence you can say positively that He, the Mighty One, has already come. He is invisible to the multitude because surrounded by the panoply of glory[6] always sent forth by the cosmic Logoi to surround an Avatar until the time for His manifestation. Yet this glory can be penetrated, under special conditions, by those who have conse-

[6] Called the Logoitic Sun.

crated themselves and given themselves up to helping wisely and silently in the great preparation. . . . These are taught how to transcend the physical and through a mighty love for humanity penetrate the glory to where their Lord waits, and correlate with Him. . . . He has come close to Earth to give comfort and help to all His children during the Day of Reckoning that is at hand—for without His presence there would be no hope—yet He can be perceived only by those who, through love and aspiration and child-like faith, can penetrate the mists of glory that surround Him; for His call still is: 'Come unto me in spirit and in truth.' His presence in the aura of the Earth brings such a mighty outpouring of Love that all who come to Him in spirit and in truth will find the comfort and help needed for themselves and also to help others. . . .

". . . Indeed, all who have faith and believe in His mighty love and catch even a ray of His radiance will be comforted and helped; for His mighty out-shining is a panoply of strength and comfort intervening between them and destruction, as the scripture saith: 'With a strong hand, and a stretched out arm; for His mercy endureth forever.' . . . He brings the glory of the Logoitic Sun, and it spreads through the ocean of humanity and gives humanity the strength to withstand the disasters that come at the end of every age.

"America has a great work to perform for the New Day. America, which is so often called the land of the free, is yet so bound, so tied down with the green withes of materalism, so helplessly caught in a net of misunderstanding and the money-question. Yet it was born to be the land of the free, and you must help to set it free, to bring about the freedom of the world. But to do so it must recognize its mystical inner power. . . .

"America is the greatest nation on Earth, and has been so destined from its inception, because it is a reincarnation of the old Atlanteans who are reincarnating at this time to do a very important service for humanity and the world. And it can save the world if it tries. Even if every one will not work for it, where two or three are gathered together in knowledge and power and persistency, in accomplishment, there can be no doubt about the result. . . . America has the power to save this world from the cataclysms and conditions which will be the turning-point toward destruction or salvation. . . .

"The great and mighty omnipotent Power, which at this day and generation is once more to send down into this dark star the great outshining of His only begotten Son, must have disciples who can touch His robe. It is the Day of Regeneration. No longer must it be a descent into the darkness of crucifixion and death. He must have disciples who know, even if they be but few, gathered from all quarters of the world, gathered in the Upper Chamber of the higher, divine intuition, knowing each other.

"These are the days prophesied of old when East and West must meet; when hands must be clasped; when the great wall of misunderstanding shall be torn down; when the East shall learn that it is not the

East alone that worships the true Lord God of Hosts, but also the sons and daughters of the West who have dedicated their lives to His service. . . .

"The time is drawing close when all centers in all lands must recognize each other and join together, every one who can lift up his hands in blessing and cry to the Lord God in any language for the blessings to descend: the blessings of understanding, of brotherhood, of oneness; the overcoming of the power of those in all countries who drive their fellow men like lambs to the slaughter. . . .

"There is going to be a period of eclipse, of darkness, when the clouds of human mind-stuff are rolling up like thunder-caps: when we hear the distant rumble of the storm: when we know there is danger: when we know we must be more and more filled with the living power of the Christ if we would save the ship. . . . This little speck we call the Earth is our ship, and it is in great distress. It is tossed hither and thither. What can save it? Only God. And what is God? He is not a Being far off in heaven. He is Divine Love. And He has placed centers of force in every human being through which His kind of love can radiate and manifest. What will you do to awaken that force, spread it and save the world? . . .

"In ages long past, when the time for a cyclic Earth change had come, there was gathered together a great company which said: 'Come, let us build a mighty temple unto the Lord.' And the great pyramid of Egypt still stands to-day as a monument to their efforts. To accomplish this there was a great burying of all differences in ideas and religious conceptions, and an overwhelming desire to embody the divine principles of the making and maintaining of the universe in such a way that it would be a lesson to all future generations.

"Every step was carefully considered, and the many types of people necessary were brought together from all parts. First there was the Prophet to whom was given the idea and its symbology, the plans and measurements, in which the wonderful hidden mysteries of the Earth were to be foreshadowed and embodied. Then came the Divine Helpers of that mortal, those who upheld the hands of the one to whom the task was given. Then there were the many classes of artisans and workers of all kinds gathered from the ends of the Earth, each a specialist in his own line, yet all agreeing to the great mandate: 'Come, let us make a mighty temple unto the Lord.'

"Then came the serfs, the ignorant ones, the laborers. These were not beaten slaves as history imagines, for no such temple could have been built or have endured through the ages on such a basis. There was not one who had not his own place and work—of mind, of talent or of body—and all this work was given freely as a sacrifice to the God of Gods. Even to-day it still is a mystery to the modern world how it was accomplished. How did they gain their superhuman knowledge, their superhuman ability? By devotion. By giving themselves to their Cause: their lives, their talents, their all. That mighty pile therefore stands to-day as a great monument, not, as we so often hear, to God's glory alone, but to *man's coöperation, devotion and determination.*

"To-day we are drawing very close to another just such a mighty era in the world's unfoldment. And the Lord Christ comes down to Earth and says: 'Build unto me another mighty pyramid which shall endure throughout the ages as a monument to my glory and to the devotion and coöperation of my children.' But this new monument is not to be made of stones and earth and cement and the particles and forces of the Earth. It is to be made of human hearts, of human lives, of human devotion. . . . What shall become of you if this day of days, this time of times, this great cosmic anniversary is waiting for recognition and fulfillment and mankind fails to grasp it? . . .

"Those who have heard the call, those who can understand and grasp the mystery of the mighty work to be accomplished are the ones to inaugurate it. You are but human and the greatness and magnitude of the work may stagger your minds and you may say: 'We are so small in the world's sight, so seemingly powerless and limited in every way, yet we will do our best.' But all can begin at the beginning. First, the preparation of their hearts to comprehend and their minds to understand the mighty ideal; second, to overcome the natural tendencies which lead them away from devoting their attention to the ideals of their inner and real life.

"This is a mighty work, and if America is to become the Heart of the World it is here that it should begin. Here its heart must begin to beat like that of an unborn babe. When a child is to be born the first sign of life is the beating of the fetal heart, and that is also the last center to cease at death. The fetal heart of this mighty living monument to the Lord Christ has already begun to beat in the heart of this nation, but it needs love and devotion and coöperation to sustain it. And so the cry goes forth as of old: 'Come, bring your talents, your love, your life, your all, and help build this living monument unto the Lord God.' You who have heard the Voice; you who have felt the heart beat are the ones to send forth the call; to instill into every heart a vision of that which is to be and a desire to help, to build, to build with your prayers and devotion and spiritual forces as well as material; for this monument is not to be a pile of masonry, but a Flaming Fire ascending to the very throne of God, purifying the whole Earth and touching the hearts of every nationality and bringing them here.

"This is a mighty message, and it needs a mighty comprehension, a mighty devotion, a consecrated, concentrated and continual prayer, and above all communion with the Lord of Nations. You cannot accomplish it alone. God Himself cannot accomplish it alone. For it is destined that His sanctuary shall be built by sanctified hearts and by hands gladly given to lift up His banner before the heart-hungry, distant, weary and despondent children. . . . Begin with this Order which you love and help to support, and build, build, build. Spread its Teachings broadcast to every awakened heart. Spread the knowledge of its books. Let there be no lack; for this is the beginning of that great Brotherhood of Nations that is to be gathered, not only out of this nation, but out of all nations, to build this mighty Temple unto the Lord God. . . . Be like that unknown king whose name has died out of history, yet who first got the conception of the pyramid. Be like those helpers who, putting into it their all, built into it the mysteries of science and religion not then even dreamed of, but which were to be manifested later. . . .

"Then pray daily that the little doors of this Heart of the World shall speedily open; that this wonderful Child of Light shall grow and wax strong and come to birth in this nation, so that all mankind shall see the Light of His countenance shining through. . . . Will you enlist in this great undertaking? Will you devote your lives, your loves, your understanding, your all, to the solving of the greatest problem the world has ever faced? to bring peace and harmony and coöperation out of the present-day confusion and unbrotherliness, that the one Divine Light may shine forth and illumine all?"

CHAPTER VI

THE BATTLE OF ARMAGEDDON[1]

"And I saw three unclean spirits like frogs come out of the mouth of the dragon, and out of the mouth of the beast, and out of the mouth of the false prophet. For they are the spirits of devils, working miracles, which go forth unto the kings of the whole earth and of the whole world, to gather them to the battle of that great day of God Almighty. . . . And he gathered them together into a place called in the Hebrew tongue Armageddon." *Revelation,* xvi, 13-16.

The literal meaning of Armageddon is "on the heights" or "on high," and in this sense it is used to designate not a physical battlefield but the invisible realms of the astral plane. The hosts which are gathered to this great battle are the hosts of the accumulated thought-forms of lust, greed, envy, hate, selfishness and unbrotherliness engendered by the wrong thinking of humanity from the beginning, as well as the *results of their evil words and deeds.*

Jeremiah specifically refers to these forces *as causes* when he says: "Hear, O earth; behold, I will bring evil upon this people, *even the fruit of their thoughts,* be-

[1] Although this chapter was first written in May, 1909, revised Sept. 10, 1914, and published in the second edition of our *Philosophy of War* in Sept., 1917, in view of the many predictions it contains—some of which have already been fulfilled—we feel justified in reprinting it in this collection of prophecies, especially as *The Philosophy of War* is now out of print. Allowance should therefore be made for the fact that it was first published seventeen years ago. —*The Authors.*

cause they have not harkened unto my words, nor my law, but rejected it." [2] During this battle all the stored-up evil must have a focus through which it can pour itself out upon the lowest or physical plane where its precipitation will end the cycle of its manifestation.

These forces have accumulated because, during the childhood of the Race, the Lords of Karma, through the Masters of Wisdom and the Rulers of the sub-races, have held the forces back until the Race grew strong enough to bear them upon its shoulders: grew up as it were. The cycle is now closing and the time for the adjustment is at hand so that the new sixth sub-race may enter the New Age with a clean slate. "Therefore I am full of the fury of the Lord (Law); I am weary with holding in: I will pour it out upon the children abroad, and upon the assembly of young men together." [2]

And there is invariably found some human being who, because of his prominence and because of his habit of opening his mind to the insinuating flattery and fatuous promises of great attainments or perhaps to world dominion from the astral leaders—whom the *Bible* refers to as "the rulers of the darkness of this world"—becomes the executor or mouthpiece of the stored-up evil forces or the channel through which they find expression in the physical world, as for instance, Nero, the Borgias, and others in later eras. In this way the evil and unredeemed Karma of the Race is adjusted so as to permit the good aspect of the forces involved to be extracted, just as ore is crushed

[2] *Jeremiah,* vi, 19, also vi, 11.

or melted that the gold may be extracted. Often such an one believes himself to be the chosen of the Lord, chosen to cleanse the world or to impose his idea of culture upon it; for the dominant Principalities of Evil have convinced him that they are the Voice of God, and he prides himself on being their obedient servant.

Hence, while many are referring to the present European conflict as Armageddon, the meaning of the word shows that the present World War is *but one reflection* or outpouring on Earth of the real battle that has been raging in the higher realms. It is precipitated now because an earthly channel has been found in the person of a leader sufficiently egotistical, presumptuous and self-righteous to listen to the flattery of the astral entities and become the earthly advocate of those powers of darkness.

The working out and adjustment of these karmic forces must take place at the close of each Race, and in a lesser degree at the close of each sub-race. This adjustment precipitates the great race wars which are followed by the cataclysms which mark the close of sub-races and Races; for every particle of the matter composing the Race-continents, as well as every particle in the body of individual man, must have its own individual balancing, purification, readjustment and ultimate redemption that it may be ready for subsequent advance.

The last great Armageddon of an entire Race occurred just before the sinking of the continent of Atlantis, at the close of the cycle of the Fourth Great Race (Atlantean). "This hints at the struggle between the 'Sons of God' and the Sons of the Dark Wisdom—our forefathers; or the Atlantean and Aryan Adepts. The whole history of that period is allegorized in the *Ramayana* which is the mystic narrative in epic form of the struggle between Rama—the first king of the Divine Dynasty of the early Aryans and the agent of the white forces—and Ravana, the symbolic personification of the Atlantean (Lanka) Race and the agent of the Black Forces. The former were incarnations of the Solar Gods; the latter, of the Lunar Devas. This was the great battle between Good and Evil, between White and Black Magic, for the supremacy of the divine forces over the lower terrestrial, or cosmic powers." [3]

The sinking of the continent of Atlantis which followed that Armageddon was the balancing of the accounts of the entire Fourth Race. It was a necessary preparation—through the purifying action of the salt water [4] of the continent for a future Race, the Sixth.

The survivors of that cataclysm—those who were sufficiently spiritualized, awakened and obedient to follow their Divine Rulers—were picked out, separated and trained by the Masters long before the sinking of the continent, and so became the seed of the present Fifth (Ayran) Great Race, just as certain people are now being chosen and trained for a similar function.

Ere this present Fifth Race ends some thousands of years hence—for we are now just entering upon its

[3] *The Secret Doctrine,* Blavatsky, ii, 520.
[4] For details see *The Voice of Isis,* Curtiss, Chapt. xxxi.

sixth sub-race[5]—a similar adjustment of its Race Karma must take place, and it has now already begun its physical manifestation. The great World War now raging offers a focal point through which the Karma of the fifth sub-race of the Aryan Race can be precipitated upon the physical plane and adjusted. And in Emperor William of Germany a leader has been found who could be so deluded and obsessed[6] as to be used as the tool of the dark forces. But we must remember the words of Jesus: "It must needs be that offences come; but woe to that man by whom the offence cometh." Therefore, while we must condemn his acts we must also pity and pray for the man.

Europe is the first focal point for Armageddon because it was in Europe that the greater part of that Karma was engendered, *i.e.*, through the many bitter political wars which drenched its soil in blood; through the sectarian wars carried on in the name of the Church, but which perverted religion and made priestcraft a curse; and through the intolerance, selfishness and mental and spiritual blindness of the religious leaders which manifested in the mental war which finally culminated in the most inhuman persecutions the civilized world has ever known—that religious frenzy known as the Inquisition.

To-day we are reaping especially the Karma sown by the unspeakable cruelties practiced by the Inquisi-

[5] *The Voice of Isis*, Curtiss, Chapt. xvii.

[6] Since this was written various officers of the Kaiser's household have testified that they have frequently seen him "under control" or obsessed, speaking in a strange voice and claiming to be the mouthpiece of God.

tion; for it stands as the great crime of the fifth subrace. While it is true that Christians were burned and tortured in the earlier centuries by Nero and others, even what are called pre-Christian atrocities were but the spawn out of which the Inquisition was hatched, and from that can be traced almost all the degrading crimes of the later days, especially intolerance and hatred and their results. We are apt to associate the Inquisition with Spain, yet Spain and her western colonies did not institute the Inquisition until the year 1232, while in Italy, France, England and Germany it was in full swing, with intervals of cessation, from early in the sixth century. Especially in Germany, with Conrad of Marburg—called the "Terrible"—as chief inquisitor, the cruelty was prosecuted with such extreme zeal and horror as even to exceed the wishes of the Pope. The Inquisition was also established on the high seas in all galleys and ships. There the cruelties and punishments were beyond belief.

While this present conflict seems wholly evil, it is not entirely so for the Race; for not only will many of the old karmic debts be adjusted, and thus allow the contending nations to enter into a federation in which the independence of each nation and people will be guaranteed[7]—as brothers, some older, some younger, in the great social family—and thus prevent war for a long period, wipe out at least part of the karmic debt and enter the new era with a clean slate, as it were, but the war is developing in the Race as a

[7] Fulfilled in the League of Nations.

whole an enormous amount of the feminine qualities —love, compassion, sympathy, devotion, unselfishness and service[8]—so necessary as the Race enters the Aquarian or Woman's Age, "the sign of the Son of Man in heaven."

Among the contending nations the English, French and Germans have reached the zenith of their cycles as nations and hence must be tested ere they can enter the new cycle. They are classed among the nations which represent the highest stage of modern civilization, culture, intellectual and material advance on the planet to-day, but they must now prove the truth of their proud boasts; must prove whether their civilization and culture is the result of true *spiritual* growth or whether it is the mere veneer of *intellectual and material* attainment, founded in cruelty and intolerance, and without corresponding *spiritual* unfoldment.[9]

Has their so-called advance in civilization brought their people into a greater realization of the *spiritual basis of all manifestation?* Has it led them to strive for a more *conscious communion* with the realms of spiritual consciousness as a daily and personal experience? Has it taught them the folly of seeking to satisfy the ceaseless craving of the Soul for *union with its Source*, through the gratification of the senses or the possession of material things? Has their scientific

[8] Exemplified in charities to stricken nations on a scale never before known in the history of mankind.

[9] Since the above was first published America entered the war as a full grown youth now assuming the great responsibilities of manhood. Hence America and her institutions must also be tested and proved by fire.

study of the wonderful coöperation and brotherhood existing among the cells, tissues and organs of every unit of organized life led them—if for no other reason, as a matter of efficiency—to follow *the same law* and express greater tolerance, coöperation and brotherhood among themselves as members of the great body of humanity? Have their studies led them to recognize the true position of woman as the Priestess of the Household, the complement and co-worker with man; the spiritual head of the family, as man is the material; the inspirer and leader in all spiritual, ethical and moral problems?

In time of emergency, stress and strain, when there is scarcely time for thought, will the culture of these nations enable them instinctively to display more love, compassion, self-sacrifice and humanity—simply because man is man—than the less cultured nations would under similar conditions? Or will they relapse to the level of the uncultured animal man who fights solely for self? *This is the test which their civilizations must stand.* And those nations which show most conclusively that these higher qualities have been built into their national consciousness must be the ones to dominate and manifest these qualities more perfectly in the world's arena during the coming cycle of the New Age.

The Slavonic nations, on the other hand, have not reached the zenith of their evolution, but are on the upward arc. Hence, the more primitive qualities of their civilization may be used by the Great Law as instruments with which to accomplish the testing of the more advanced nations, and to make possible the inauguration of the New Era.

When the physical conflict is over a terrible mental revolt against all forms of restraint, both in government and religion, will burst forth.[10] It will be a period of extremes, extremes of individualism; a period when the opposition to all systematized or organized spiritual teachings, which is even now manifesting under various doctrines of religious and so-called "soul freedom," will find extreme expression.

It will be a period both of extreme agnosticism and extreme individualistic teaching, when any fantastic theory, even without a rational or philosophic basis, will find a hearing and followers. At the same time there will be a strong feeling upon the part of those who cling to the old conceptions that it is their duty to humanity to enforce the old religious ideals.[11] *This will be a great test as to whether religious intolerance has been outgrown;* for there can be no permanent peace until the minds of a majority of mankind have been sufficiently developed, broadened and spiritualized to banish it forever.

Hence, all churches, orders, movements and societies professing a spiritual basis will on the one hand have radicals whose extremes will bring them into disrepute, while on the other hand they will have those who will laugh at, ridicule, discredit, oppose and persecute them.

[10] Since this was first published (1914), it has already begun its fulfillment through the action of the Bolsheviki, but they will not be the only ones.

[11] Fulfilled in the strife between the Fundamentalists and Modernists, the Scopes' and other "evolution trials," etc.

And the same fire that has manifested as physical war *will again sweep the world* as a mental, spiritual and psychic conflict, and it is always those nearest and dearest or those companions who helped us create the Karma, who are used by the Great Law to test us and adjust the Karma.

It will be a time when all spiritual movements will be under a cloud; when spiritually "The brother shall betray the brother to death, and the father the son: and children shall rise against their parents, and shall cause them to be put to death."[12] Therefore, it will be a period of great testing; a period when every heart who has realized the reality of the spiritual world and its forces must be securely grounded in the philosophy, and stand firmly and unshakably for his or her beliefs, even though to do so involves ridicule, persecution and mental suffering. For every system of teaching not founded upon the rock of Divine Reality and expressed in terms suitable to the new conditions must pass away to make room for the new.

These conditions will be so terrible that they will last only a very few years, perhaps only two or three, for we are told that "for the elect's sake those days shall be shortened. . . . And except those days should be shortened, there should be no flesh saved." The only way that the "elect" can prove themselves is by their sincerity, their steadfastness, their trust and their determination to hold calmly to their spiritual ideals and *to rely absolutely upon their divine inner guidance,*

[12] *St. Mark,* xiii, 12.

while they *pray without ceasing* that these days be shortened.

Words and arguments will be of no avail. The truth of their beliefs can be proved only by living them. All such will be like bright and shining lights in this period of mental and spiritual darkness, or more correctly, blindness. It will not be until *after the close of this period* that the long-expected Great Teacher, the Avatar, will appear to reassure distracted humanity of the *spiritual basis of all manifestation,* and to outline a new and higher conception of the spiritual life and its forms of expression.

The battles of the physical world are fought on the physical plane with physical weapons, but the true Battle of Armageddon must be fought first upon the astral plane with thoughts and psychic forces for weapons, the conflict now raging being but a pouring out of the evil and a gathering together of the forces of Good for the final battle on the higher planes.

This battle has already begun. And during the entire sixth sub-race of the present Fifth Great Race we may expect more or less unsettled conditions. For this is the time of adjustment; the time of struggle to overcome the evils which the Race as a whole has outlived, yet which it has not fully conquered and redeemed. The number 6 is both the number of the Christ [13] and also of unrest. It symbolizes the mighty struggle of the Christ-force to penetrate into and transmute the evil and manifest itself. Hence, only as humanity enters into the seventh sub-race will it have true and

[13] For details see *The Key to the Universe,* Curtiss, 195.

lasting peace and rest, although groups here and there may have it before that time; for God blessed the seventh day and hallowed it—also the seventh Race, and each seventh sub-race, is especially blessed—and during that period rested from His labors.

Therefore, the progress of the sixth sub-race into which we are now entering will be marked by tremendous disasters precipitated upon the physical plane [14]—wars, earthquakes, cyclones, volcanic eruptions and meteoric showers, floods, etc.—of more or less severity until the final battle and cataclysm in which the battlefield and the defeated army will be swallowed up and a new and purified land shall arise out of the waters, during the sixth sub-race, for the new Sixth Great Race to inhabit. The victors will remain as the seed of the New Race to people the new land.

The "final battle" does not refer to the end of this present war of nations, but to the close of the true Battle of Armageddon of which the present war *is but the first phase.* The cataclysmic changes in the Earth's surface will result in the rising out of the waters of the Pacific ocean the ancient Lemurian continent which, during the entire seventh sub-race, will pass through the various steps [15] necessary to make it a fit dwelling place for the Sixth Great Race.

Just as these changes must take place for the planet, so must they take place in humanity through bloody wars, strikes and other conflicts which will continue

[14] First published in 1909.

[15] For details see *The Voice of Isis,* Curtiss, 388.

until all conflicts of man with man, and man's resistance to the Divine, are swallowed up, and out of the waters of affliction there shall arise a new and greater humanity with true Brotherhood, Love, Peace and Harmony as its watchword.

The time has now come when the accumulated mass of old Race Karma must be definitely met and conquered ere humanity can enter upon the new sub-race, its next step in evolution. This accumulated Karma, in a measure, is to the world what the Dweller on the Threshold is to the neophyte. And, as with the neophyte before each important step is taken, it must be met and conquered. For just as the neophyte, through his evil thoughts, words and acts, has created an entitized form of evil—his individual Dweller—so humanity has been pouring out its evils throughout its long cycle until they have become entitized as a "dark planet" with a living Ruler, the Anti-Christ, who definitely works through those who give themselves up to his guidance or obsession. This dark planet may be called the Dweller on the Threshold for humanity as a whole.

The astronomers of Harvard University have already discovered the influence of this dark planet [16]—the De-

[16] This prophecy has recently (1917), been strikingly confirmed by Dr. W. W. Campbell, Director of Lick Observatory who, in explaining why there were sudden black gaps or "holes" in the giant star clusters around which there was "a high density of star distribution right up to the sharply defined edges of the holes and yet leave the holes empty of stars," stated in his remarks on the Nebulæ that "he was inclined to assume, with Barnard and others, that the stars are actually there and that they are invisible, because *invisible materials between us and the stars* are absorbing or hiding the light

stroyer—which, if encountered, means the destruction of the Earth. Astronomer Serviss is quoted as saying that the Earth and this whole solar system has gone astray and is trailing off away from its path around the great sun Alcyone in the Pleiades, toward the constellation Andromeda in the Milky Way. These are but astronomical confirmations of the fact that we have entered the sixth sub-race, and that the hosts are rapidly gathering for the great Battle of Armageddon. The Earth is being driven through space in this new direction by the character of the thought-force of its collective humanity.

But there is another planet, not yet recognized by science, which is a bright planet—the Redeemer—to be drawn into whose aura means salvation. These two planets may be called the camping grounds of the opposing forces, with the Earth as the battle-ground.

But back of and within the outer cause, as the propelling power, will be the preponderating force of good or evil thoughts engendered by humanity. Therefore, the real battle is to be fought on the mental and astral planes with thoughts and psychic forces, good and bad, as weapons, and later will be reflected and precipitated on and in the Earth. Hence, all advanced students who consciously determine to make Love, Brotherhood,

which the stars are trying to send to us." . . . The so-called new stars afford interesting evidence on this point. *These are stars which suddenly flash out at points where previously no stars were known to exist* . . . a temporary star is seemingly best examined on the theory that *a dark or relatively dark star* travelling rapidly through space has met with resistance."

Purity and Peace their standards of life, thus enroll themselves among the Hosts of the Lord and become Soldiers of the Cross.

The Earth, also humanity, is purified alternately by water and fire, and both are now passing through a baptism of fire. Every soldier in the armies, as well as every munition worker and helper behind the lines, is helping the Great Law to bring this purifying process into manifestation. Hence, each one is a servant of the Divine Flame and is helping to work out a cosmic event in the evolution of mankind, whether he or she knows it or not.

The Dragon of the text quoted at the head of this chapter symbolizes the synthesis of the world's perverted thoughts of sex and is commonly called the Devil. The three unclean spirits like frogs which come from his mouth symbolize the three great expressions of the dragon-force, *i.e.,* (a) sex impurity, suppression and perversion; (b) the creation of disease by such perversion, and (c) extreme cruelty, frightfulness and insanity or psychic obsession resulting from astral entities—or individual Dwellers on the Threshold—utilizing sensitive but negative victims through which they can satisfy their desires.[17]

The Beast is a symbol of Mammon or greed, expressing through the Money Power. The three evil spirits issuing from his mouth comprise all the miseries and sorrows that arise as a result of greed and injustice in their threefold expressions of (a) war, prosecuted

[17] For full details as to obsession and its prevention and cure and all after-death conditions see *Realms of the Living Dead,* Curtiss.

for territorial or commercial expansion, stimulated and financed by the Money Power; (b) poverty, resulting from the unjust distribution of wealth, which distribution is controlled by the Money Power; and (c) all the train of evils resulting from bodily and industrial slavery.

The False Prophet symbolizes all false teachings which have been given out in the name of religion or spiritual teaching to justify and uphold both the Dragon and the Beast, but which have misled humanity and held it back from manifesting Peace, Love and Brotherhood. From his mouth come forth the three frogs of (a) materialized religion, priestcraft, temporal power and world dominion; (b) spiritual pride; and (c) intolerance and its handmaiden, religious persecution.

This conflict of pride, intolerance and persecution did not die out with the Inquisition, but is still active to-day. It is now directed not so much against the physical bodies of its victims, but is conducted mentally and psychically through the slanders, scandals and malicious misrepresentations carried on through various publications and commonly called "brutal journalism." All these factors, as the *Bible* passage quoted plainly tells us, work for King Desire and his allies and their cohorts.

One of the first rules impressed upon the spiritual aspirant is that to attain at-one-ment by the Path of Love and Purity he must lay down all carnal weapons. Jesus emphasized this rule when He said to Peter: "Put up again thy sword into his place: for all they that take the sword shall perish with the sword."[18] Yet we find the disciple spoken of as a Soldier of the Cross and commanded to array himself as a fighting factor in the world's salvation. Jesus also said: "I came not to send peace, but a sword."[19] Behind this paradox lies a great truth, the understanding of which is necessary ere any decided conscious advance in the spiritual unfoldment of either the individual or the Race can take place, *i.e.*, the conquering must take place on the plane where the causes were engendered, and the weapons are Love and Purity.

This means that thoughts and prayers of Love and Purity must be sent out in such numbers *and with such positive spiritual force* that they will surround and transmute the impure and antagonistic forces, following the same tactics as the white warrior cells (phagocytes) of the blood use in meeting an invasion of disease germs, *i.e.*, not deny the evil, but *surround and transmute* the evil into good. *The Voice of the Silence* tells us: "Strive with thy thoughts unclean before they overpower thee. Use them *as they will thee*, for if thou sparest them and they take root and grow, know well these thoughts will overpower and kill thee."[20] If you find them persistently clinging to you, send out an army of pure and loving thoughts to absorb and transmute them.

Science recognizes the fact that, during epidemics of disease, the mere thinking and talking about the disease

[18] *St. Matthew*, xxvi, 52.
[19] *St. Matthew*, x, 34.
[20] *The Voice of the Silence*, Blavatsky, 12.

will make negative persons more susceptible to it. This does not mean that all disease is merely mental—the fact that animals are swept with infectious diseases disproves that—but that by negative thoughts we open a door in our aura through which the disease can enter. This effect is still more evident in moral epidemics and in the epidemics of war-thoughts which sweep over nations, or unconsidered action sweeps a mob. Therefore, the spiritual aspirant, while fighting steadfastly for Justice and Righteousness, should lay down all carnal thoughts of hatred and revenge or he will surely "perish with the sword," overcome by the hosts of evil thought-forms he has drawn into his aura.

Applied to warring nations this principle indicates that we should not waste time and force in directing our prayers and thought-forces to specific European nations that they shall cease fighting, for they are acting under the tremendous urge of long pent-up karmic readjustment *which must take place,* and they cannot respond to our prayers until after the karmic readjustment has been worked out. As well might we sit down and pray that a dirty room might be swept and cleaned without any action on our part. The result can be accomplished only by the power of the housemaid's broom.

There is only one efficacious way to pray for peace and that is to pray that the Will of the Father shall be done on Earth—even *as it is done* in heaven—through those who can understand, respond to and execute that Will. That divine Will is Love first, last and all the time. And having prayed thus we must believe and know that this Divine Love is back of the entire world of manifestation, and that it is ever working to bring about the reign of universal Love, Peace and Harmony, even though it be necessary to sweep from its path all that opposes that reign.

The terrible conditions which prevail to-day[21] are not the Will of the Father, but are the creations of man; the result of his *resistance and opposition* to the Divine Will; the creations of unbrotherliness, ambition, selfishness and greed, not altogether on the part of those instrumental in precipitating and now participating in the present conflict, but the accumulation of selfishness and greed of the Race, all of which must come up for adjustment now at the close of the cycle of the fifth sub-race, which is also the end of the old Piscean dispensation, just as the rash must come out in measles, scarlet fever, etc., ere the real healing can begin.

Therefore, while we *pray that these days be shortened*, know well that Peace and Righteousness *must first come in the hearts* of the people *of all the nations involved* and of the whole world. Arms and amunition are but harmless and inert physical things and without the power to initiate injury or destruction; *it is only man's will to use them for such purposes* that makes them dangerous.

Try not to think of individuals except in compassion, knowing that the Great Law will adjust their con-

[21] September 15, 1917.

ditions in its own good time. Those who are dying for their ideals, even those whose ideals are but of local patriotism and loyalty to an earthly ruler, are in a measure redeemers for the Race; for they are dying that the Race may be purged from the war-thought, the war-ideal and the curse of militarism. Hence, in their next incarnation they will receive the just reward for their sacrifice.

By their suffering and dying they have brought the world to a greater realization of the utter folly and needlessness of war if the Divine Will were followed; for there is nothing that so counteracts the idea of war as to have a dearly loved one killed in such a war. By their sacrifice they have wiped out much of the individual and racial Karma and will receive their compensation by being enabled to incarnate the next time very quickly—even now, perhaps through the same mothers—and under far more advanced conditions of civilization than they could have experienced had they remained a few years longer in the present life. Those who die with hatred in their hearts and while consciously opposing the reign of Righteousness will remain out of incarnation for a long, long cycle; in fact, until the Race has learned how to deal with them.

Send your forces of Love, Peace and Brotherhood into the higher realms where they will aggregate into a mighty force which will swallow up all future thoughts of national selfishness and aggrandizement and be a powerful factor in forming a federation[22] of Euro-

[22] Partially fulfilled in the League of Nations.

pean nations on the grounds of common humanity and brotherhood which shall make it impossible for the ambitions or passions of a few to plunge nations into bloody and needless conflicts, and which should be an important factor in preparing for the coming of the Avatar.

All persons who are sensitive have realized for some time that there is a terrible commotion in the mental and astral worlds which is now intensified by the physical conflict going on in Europe, and also by the thousands of Souls which have suddenly been thrown out of incarnation, some of whom carry with them all the excitement, antagonism and hatred which animated them as they fought.[23] This composite force is like a tension or a steady pressure upon all humanity, tending to make all persons more irritable and excited. Therefore, it is the duty of every advanced student to take special pains to see that he does not make an opening in his aura through which such forces can manifest by giving way to impatience, irritation and emotion or to partisanship, race- and class-antagonism. Instead, he should *consciously strive to make himself a center* from and through which the constructive forces of Peace, Harmony, Love and Brotherhood can radiate in his family and immediate environment and on out into all the world.

Arrayed against the hosts of evil stand the thought-creations of Love, Harmony, Justice, Righteousness, Purity and upliftment of the Race sent out in a steady

[23] For a full explanation of all after-death conditions see *Realms of the Living Dead,* Curtiss.

stream by the Lodge of Masters and by all Great Teachers since the world began, as well as by all persons who have been able to think *vitalized* thoughts of Love, Purity, Harmony and Brotherhood. All humanity have added and are still adding their quota to one side or the other.

It is the destiny of this fifth sub-race to see the beginning of this great and decisive battle between Good and evil or, to be more explicit, between Purity and impurity, selfishness and unselfishness. Hence it is time that all who desire the salvation of the Race and the planet should awaken to the grave conditions we have outlined herein, and *determinedly array themselves* on the side of Good by sending their individual, pure and vital love-thoughts to swell the Hosts of the Lord. For you cannot say a loving word or do a loving deed, even to an animal or plant, without having a loving thought behind it. And every loving and peaceful thought adds strength to the Army of Good. As the Christ says: "Inasmuch as ye have done it unto one of the last of these my brethren, ye have done it unto me."

The pure Hosts of the Lord are mustered in serried ranks according to natural law and order, while the forces of evil, being a perversion of nature and abnormal, are not organized in the astral world except into individual bands loosely held together only by selfish interest and ready at any moment to turn upon each other. A well-known principle of warfare is that a small but well-organized army can overcome a much larger force that is unorganized. And as evil and impure forces are sent out by haphazard impulse they may be compared to an unorganized mob, while thoughts of Good, because they require will and intention, are consciously created and can be gathered together by the Masters and formed into a well-drilled, well-disciplined and well-officered army, always in good fighting condition. Good is stronger than evil because it is constructive and immortal and works in harmony with the Great Law.

The Masters of the Great White Lodge,[24] although few in numbers as compared with the multitudes of humanity, are, nevertheless, able to engender and consciously use a far greater degree of creative force on the side of Purity, Peace, Love and Brotherhood. But even They must work with the Law as Karma, and may not forcibly prevent a Race or sub-race from experiencing its karmic retribution and readjustment. But Their efforts, being consciously directed and wisely applied, weigh heavily in the scale. They do not act on the physical plane, however, except through Their disciples and those who respond to Their inspiring currents of force. Hence, Their great need to-day is of those who will consciously make themselves centers of Peace, Purity, Harmony and Love and be more or less conscious instruments through which They can work.

Therefore, instead of devoting all your efforts toward unfolding your own faculties and developing your own personality, set to work earnestly and consciously *to create warrior thought-forces* for the Army of the

[24] For description see *The Voice of Isis,* Curtiss, 53, 187.

Lord to the end that not only you, but the Race and the planet itself, shall be saved from destruction."[25] (Written in May, 1909. Revised Sept. 30th, 1914, and Sept. 15th, 1917.)

[25] During the World War, after *The Order of Christian Mystics* had inaugurated a world-wide noon-day prayer service for peace among its students throughout the world, the idea was taken up by many churches and other organizations and within a few weeks the lust for war and the will to fight of the Central Powers was neutralized and overcome by the Will for Peace thus consciously generated. The Central Powers then made overtures for an armistice, not because they could not have fought on for months, as far as guns, ammunition and supplies were concerned, but because of a so-called "loss of morale," both in the ranks and at home. This was purely a psychological reaction to deliberately and consciously generated mass-thought action which produced the concrete result which saved millions of human lives and reshaped history and human destiny.

CHAPTER VII

THE REMEDY

"Now go, write it before them in a table, and note it in a book, that it may be for the time to come for ever and ever: that this is a rebellious people. lying children, children that will not hear the law of the Lord: which say to the seers, See not; and to the prophets, Prophesy not unto us right things, speak unto us smooth things, prophesy deceits: get you out of the way, turn aside and out of the path, cause the Holy One of Israel to cease from before us." *Isaiah,* xxx, 8-11.

"O Earth, that is sobbing, like a child in its sleep!
O Brother, who suffers with pain fierce and deep!
Stand still in the ruin your passions have wrought.
Take count of the guerdon greed and sorrow have brought.
If your heart sinks despairing in the mystical calm,
List to God's choir; its echoes bring balm.
The fire but purifies; strife ends in peace.
Hosanna! hosanna! the carnage must cease.
Lift up your voices, the day is at hand.
No more of sorrow to this happy land."
Harriette Augusta Curtiss in *Realms of the Living Dead,* 176.

Prayer is an innate instinct in the human Soul and common alike to the savage and the most cultured and intellectual of mankind. It is, therefore, as natural for man to pray—especially in times of crisis which transcend the power of man to cope with—as to breathe or think. According to the circumstances and the intellectual and spiritual development of the individual, prayer may mean intercession, protection, consecration, devotion, thanksgiving or appeal. In this case we are asking our readers to unite in prayer, not because they have been frightened at the prospect of the coming changes, not to save their own lives nor even their Souls, but to help generate such a constructive spiritual power as will counteract the evil and destructive forces and thus help to save humanity from the suffering through which it must pass if the destructive forces are not neutralized. If the united prayers of a community can produce rain and break a disastrous drouth, as has been proved generation after generation for untold ages,[1] why not apply the same law of mass-prayer to avert other and more overwhelming calamities?

In the previous chapters we have outlined the laws of the cyclic changes of the Earth's surface, and also the effects of the vibrations of humanity's thought-forces upon those changes, sufficiently for the reader to realize *the responsibility of mankind* for the conditions of suffering through which we all have to pass. But if our unchecked and unregulated thought-forces are capable of producing such terrible results, how great is the power of our thought-forces, prayers and aspirations *when consciously used* in a constructive

[1] "Less than twenty-four hours after the residents of Rockhill, S. C., had joined in the last of a series of prayer meetings to implore relief from drouth, a fifteen-minute shower fell to-day. It was the first time rain had fallen here in sixty-five days." *The Washington Post,* June 13, 1926.

On June 24, 1924, the Authors attended the dance to invoke rain held by the Indians of the pueblo of San Juan, N. M. Although the sky was cloudless when we arrived and there had been no rain for many weeks, after only the first of the series of three dances *the first shower fell,* turning the heavy coat of dust on our auto into a coating of mud!

manner! And especially when concentrated upon the manifestation of certain high and constructive ideas deliberately held at the same time each day by hundreds and thousands of earnest thinkers in all parts of the world! It is in the effort to arouse such a world-wide coördinated thinking and praying concentrated upon the one idea that *these days shall be shortened* that this little volume is put forth in the simple faith that it will accomplish much towards the desired end.

The great point is that while these changes are inevitable ultimately, they can take place gradually and harmoniously, giving mankind time to adapt itself to them without too great loss, or they can take place rapidly and destructively, according as harmony and coöperation or inharmony and antagonism is the key-note sounded by mankind as a whole.

As we said in *The Philosophy of War*: [2] "In the biblical description of those days through which the planet is passing, it is written that 'Except those days should be shortened, there should be no flesh saved: but for the elect's sake *those days shall be shortened.*' Who are the Elect for whose sake these days of tribulation and retribution shall be shortened? They are those Souls who, while recognizing the terrible karmic conditions through which humanity and the globe is passing, nevertheless bravely give of all they have, their loved ones, their treasure, their help in every way, with a realization that there is a power given them to shorten

[2] *The Philosophy of War*, Curtiss, 9, 17-18, 2nd Ed., 6 (now out of print).

these days. What does this mean? for it has a mighty mystic power. It is the power of your prayers, of your interest, of your life, of your full comprehension of that which is transpiring. . . . If you raise your hands in supplication day after day and night after night, never forgetting the terror the world is passing through and the power of the Christ to conquer all conditions when truly invoked, *these days shall be shortened.* But you must elect yourselves to be the shorteners of these days. . . .

"For the world is going mad, one class ignoring the suffering of another class; one class mad with sudden wealth, gaiety and frivolity; another class mad with poverty, sacrifice, suffering and horror. Keep your minds balanced and poised, and keep others from going to extremes. Pray for the sanity and normal balance of the world. Talk it. Preach it. Pray for it."

And to-day pray for *Brotherhood, Coöperation* and *World Harmony* between individuals, classes, nations and peoples. As one student wrote us: "Thus more and more do we gain the realization, through your Teachings, of these grand truths, and more and more do we see that much depends upon us who would elect ourselves to become the Disciples of the Living Christ to shorten the time of His coming."

That the power of public prayer cannot only bring rain in time of great need, but that the aroused public mind can quickly bring about the settlement of great national problems is evidenced by the speedy settlement (May, 1926) of the great general strike in England. And the same aroused public opinion could just as quickly settle the matter of the injustice done the Indian in this country, as well as the internal conflicts now raging in other countries, and thus speedily stop the terrifically destructive forces generated by classes and whole nations conflicting in selfish and petty strife while the fate, not only of nations, but of all humanity and the planet itself, hangs in the balance!

While we do not care to prophesy in the field of politics we may say in general that changes in government—even in this country—will naturally follow the cataclysms and will be quite as widespread and surprising. Already at the time of this writing (June 1st, 1926) three revolutions are in full swing—in Poland, Portugal and China—with a ministerial crisis in Egypt, and there is scarcely a stable government in Europe; scarcely a premier and cabinet whose tenure of office is secure.[3] Therefore, of all times in history, this is no time for further conflicts and wars, but a time for peace, prayer, harmony and coöperation among nations if they would not destroy themselves. Striving

[3] "Today, eight years after the armistice, we are living amid conditions essentially like those before the war. There has not been a single peaceful year since the peace treaty was signed. Instead, there has been fighting in Russia, China, Poland, the Balkans, Africa, and Asia Minor. And it is even said that at one time just after the great war 25 small wars were being waged simultaneously. . . .

The fact that small wars are still occurring on an average of four or five a year and that it is still possible to predict another great war after the close of the greatest and most disastrous war in history is in itself a very alarming fact. It shows that humanity has learned very little. It is clear evidence that the causes of war have not been uprooted. John Bakeless, in *The Washington Star*, July 11, 1926.

for national aggrandizement and supremacy [4] must be changed into striving for universal accord, peace and good-will, each helping the others to make the most of their resources, location and abilities for the good of all, instead of the reverse.

As the Master recently told us: "The time has come when the power of coöperation and harmony among nations; when real Brotherhood and Divine Love must and shall rule and the mind and its ambitions shall obey; when Divine Love shall be dominant; when the illumined mind shall be Its servant and eager to do Its will. The powers of destruction are preparing to manifest in a tremendous way on the Earth's surface. Therefore, *special efforts must be put forth* to radiate Peace, Harmony and Brotherhood in such floods of radiant energy that it shall neutralize the evil and minimize the destructive character of the coming changes. If this great lesson can be really learned and manifested and put into daily practice by even a small portion of humanity the whole world can pass through the coming great crossing over of the Earth's forces and really enter the Aquarian Age quickly and without one-half the catastrophes and destruction that will be absolutely necessary if this great lesson remains unlearned."

With the thought clearly held in mind that *these days shall be shortened* we can work toward that definite end. Realize that *prayers thus consciously and understandingly used* are not mere sequences of pious words, but are a definite means of invoking Spiritual Fire and providing channels through which it can mani-

[4] See page 50.

fest in humanity. Even Divine Love cannot be imposed upon humanity. Man, made in God's image, has within him the possibilities of manifesting all the God-powers, but he, himself, must open the doors through which they can manifest on Earth. Therefore, Divine Love can find expression on Earth only as the hearts of mankind voluntarily open themselves to its influx and manifestation. No need to ask God to save humanity from the results of its own creating. *It is humanity itself that must save itself through the manifestation of its God-powers* which are always ready at hand to be invoked and used *by those who will make the effort,* else humanity could never gain self-mastery.

In September, 1922, at a time when there was an acute and almost hopeless crisis in the world's affairs, we sent broadcast throughout the world a little leaflet entitled *A Prayer for World Harmony,* and in this connection we cannot do better than to reproduce what we said therein.

A PRAYER FOR WORLD HARMONY

"From the present (1921) outlook of world conditions we may calculate that the first period of readjustment, 'an hour,' will see the readjustment of capital and labor, which is *quite likely to come to a tremendous crisis soon* . . . the second phase, 'a day,' may well be the struggle for the political and social readjustments now taking place. . . . The third phase, 'a month,' will embrace the great upheaval, and consequent strife and struggle which is unavoidable in the *overturning and readjustment of religious conceptions,* teachings and thoughts on spiritual subjects."—*The Message of Aquaria,* Curtiss, 242-3.

The whole world is to-day passing through a dense smothering cloud of karmic[5] dust which has accumulated through ages of wrong thinking and acting, wrong conceptions of the Law of Life. And, alas, many are letting this dust so blind the eyes of their understanding that they believe that only through extreme selfishness, retaliation and revenge can they end their injustice and suffering; that only as the Earth is drenched with the blood of their fellow men can peace, brotherhood, justice and prosperity reign. This idea is being so systematically propagated among the unthinking masses that *unless some positive effort is made* by those who know the *Law of Life* (harmony and co-operation), those who see and feel and know that all such separative and destructive ideas will only result in a prolongation of the same conditions from which mankind has suffered so long, together with all those who desire better conditions, all united in a persistent effort to make a firm stand on *the principles of harmony and interdependence,* which we see exemplified among the various organs of our bodies, *the world is destined to rehearse once more* the terrible drama of destruction, death and suffering unspeakable which it has already passed through in so many previous cyclic periods of revolution inaugurated in the name of freedom and reform.

Since man's material evolution has steadily increased his ability to intensify the punishment he metes out to his brother man—and hence ultimately to himself—in the name of "brotherhood," and since the very dust of

[5] *Karma,* the Law of Cause and Effect.

the Earth cries out, "How long, O Lord, how long?" we call upon all well-wishers of humanity throughout the world, especially those who are beginning to sense the chill breath of the coming terror, to unite with us to "lift up their gates" and let in the King of Glory, that through the outshining of His radiance they may have power to help transmute the clouds of inharmony now hanging over mankind and avert the disasters which otherwise will naturally follow; for *conditions never right themselves,* they are righted only through the *definite constructive action* of certain persons or groups of persons who understand and unite to work wisely toward definite ends.

Firstly, we must systematically spread the idea that it is *wrong principles* and *rules of life* we are to combat, not persons or peoples; that we cannot reform another person or nation until we have carefully searched in our own hearts and in our own nation for our faults and have recognized and shown a willingness to correct them. We must also continually spread the idea that force, coercion, revenge, hatred, cruelty, *even the repetition of and clinging to the memory of wrongs we have suffered,* are destructive forces which *can only add to and never heal* the wounds from which all the world is groaning together to-day.

The first to work definitely with the Spiritual Powers which are seeking to lift up the gates of ignorance and inculcate the constructive principles of the *Law of Life* should be those advanced students whose consciousness can grasp and realize this Law and its applications, as they have been set forth by

The Order of Christian Mystics in the wide scope and variety of its philosophical and spiritual books and teachings.

Just as during the Great War we were the first to inaugurate a world-wide daily Noon Prayer-service for the triumph of right and justice, which we feel had a great psychological effect in shortening the days of carnage—for it was largely a psychological breakdown or loss of morale which brought the war to such a sudden end—so we again ask our students in all parts of the world, together with all who are willing to join with them, to repeat morning, noon and night, or oftener, but at least at noon each day, the following *Prayer for World Harmony* with a deep heart-felt realization of its significance and a scientific understanding of its dynamic psychological power to awaken *and stimulate into action* every germ of good in the hearts of mankind—the love, the compassion, the justice, coöperation and all constructive forces, and thus neutralize and transmute the evil—that the terrible rising tide of unrest, selfishness, racial and class antagonism, labor troubles and religious bigotry and intolerance, among individuals, classes and nations, may be so transmuted, or at least turned aside, that it will not find expression in a new series of armed conflicts and bloodshed, or destructive cataclysms.

The uniting of thousands of hearts and minds to this definite end should generate a great current of dynamic spiritual force sweeping continuously around the world—for it is noon somewhere every minute of the day—which like a refreshing breeze should cool the heat of conflicting interests and blow off the karmic dust of the past which is settling upon and blinding individuals and nations to the *Law of Life*—harmony and coöperation. Thus shall we be of practical psychological help in opening wide "the everlasting doors" and preparing for the quick coming of the King of Glory, not only into our own hearts and lives, but into the lives of nations and humanity as a whole.

Remember that the battle which is still raging in the world is *a battle of principles,* and that the *Law of Life* must ultimately prevail. But it will prevail only after terrible calamities and renewed suffering to individuals, classes and nations *unless they unite* to lift up their gates and permit the King of Glory to come in and help them transmute the clouds of karmic dust and inharmony into peace, brotherhood and coöperation.

See the Radiance which this Prayer invokes, dispelling the clouds of inharmony as the Sun dispels the fog, and stimulating the growth of the good in each heart as the Sun stimulates the growth of the sprout when the fog has been dispelled and the Sun can carry on its constructive work.

PRAYER FOR WORLD HARMONY

Glory and honor and worship be unto Thee, O Lord Christ,[6] *Thou who art the Life and Light of all mankind!*

Thou art the King of Glory to whom all the peoples of the Earth should give joyful allegiance and service.

Inspire mankind with a realization of true Brotherhood.

Teach us the wisdom of peace, harmony and co-operation.

Breathe into our hearts the understanding that only as we see ourselves as parts of the one body of humanity can peace, harmony, success and plenty descend upon us.

Help us to conquer all manifestations of inharmony and evil in ourselves and in the world.

May all persons and classes and nations cease their conflicts, and unselfishly strive for peace and good-will, that the days of tribulation may be shortened.

Bless us all with the Radiance of Thy divine Love and Wisdom that we may ever worship Thee in the beauty of holiness.

In the Name of the Living Christ we ask it. Amen.

[6] Meaning the highest spiritual Ideal, which all nations worship under one name or another.

It is understood, of course, that *The Order of Christian Mystics* does not attribute to the *Prayer for World Harmony* entire credit for all the constructive steps toward international coöperation and world harmony, but those results following so quickly as an apparent fulfillment of the very points mentioned in that Prayer, and we having had ample proof of the reality and power of the mental and spiritual forces generated by such a Prayer, especially when directed by this Order, we feel perfectly justified in assuming that the *Prayer for World Harmony,* repeated daily by hundreds of students in all lands, did have an important psychological effect upon the minds and hearts of those leaders of nations who achieved the above results, sometimes by a change of front over night. And even if the Near East Conference should fail entirely and the karmic Flame of War mentioned in the *Prophecy of the King of the World* should sweep from East to West and affect every country, even then we will have done our best to arouse mankind to generate the spiritual forces necessary to neutralize and counteract such a disaster. So let us not be discouraged at any set-backs or cease our efforts for the salvation of mankind from such a catastrophe.

As we said in our *Prayer for the Allies* in 1917: "The concentration of the minds and hearts of thousands of advanced students in many lands who understand the power and reality of the currents of force generated by thought, aspiration, love and will for righteousness, will cause such an outpouring of creative thought- and love-force that it shall rise like incense into the higher realms and rain down upon the hearts and minds of humanity with such quickening power as to fructify every mind capable of grasping and responding to the idea which the Prayer embodies, and vivifying them into action." [7]

In a recent message from the Teacher of *The Order of Christian Mystics* we are told that:

"This is the day given you to prepare. Cry it from the housetops to those who know and can understand. The Day is at hand. Shall it be a day of great peace, of wonderful illumination? a majority of Christ-illumined ones? or shall it be another cycle of darkness more terrible than any that has passed in the world's history? For much has been given to mankind and much will be required. Even to the worldly ones much has been given: great understanding has been poured forth. Out of mighty tribulation much is sensed and comprehended, hence much is required.

"If this generation fails, then the whole system must pass once more down into the darkness from which so laboriously it is emerging. A blank ignorance will oppress humanity. Cruelty and a deliberate turning from the Light will wipe out all that civilization has attained. Chaos will reign among people. This mighty land, called the land of the free, will be a land of slaves. Art and literature will be destroyed and forgotten. Great inventions that are only waiting for proper conditions to come forth for the benefit of humanity will be smothered in birth. . . . Look on the

[7] *The Philosophy of War,* Curtiss, 2nd Ed., 6 (now out of print).

two pictures and decide where you stand. It is as though you were called to follow the colors. What will *you* do to save the world? Remember, it is not your own Souls, but the world you must save.

"There is great power in the faith of even a few repeating the words. Say, 'The more I believe a thing; the more I repeat it; the more I send it out and the more people see and follow it, the more the powers of the universe . . . will carry it to the ends of the earth.' Send out your thoughts like living fire that will penetrate into every crevice and cell in the body of the nation. . . . But you must be earnest and constant and daily, always at the same hour if possible."

By such invocations we are filling not only ourselves, but also the reservoirs of the Earth—the vast caverns and the arched passageways—full to overflowing with Spiritual Fire whose radio-active emanations will neutralize and consume the inharmonies and evils that mankind has generated and thus shorten the days of tribulation. Mourn not, therefore, for the Earth or its inhabitants, knowing that whatever comes is but the result of the Divine Flame bursting through our limitations and resistance to bring to us a new realization that only Divine Love, manifesting as true Brotherhood, Harmony and Coöperation, can bring peace, happiness and perfection.

The above prophecy presents the picture as it stands to-day on the Screen of Time, but we are told that for the Elects' sake these days shall be shortened. The results depend upon the reaction of humanity and the activity of the Elect. Worry and fear only add to the world's misery, while every happy, trusting heart sows seeds of happiness and trust in the hearts of others. Those who elect to help shorten these days should send out their aspiration, love and compassion in constant prayer.

Therefore, we ask all who will to use some such prayer as our *Prayer for World Harmony* morning, noon and night, and *spread this idea as widely as possible* that its vibrations may affect and inspire the hearts of all mankind, and particularly the leaders of nations. The use of this Prayer or mantram will not only have a psychological effect, according to the mental and spiritual force we put into it and the persistency and positive will with which we repeat it, but it will also form an avenue in the body of humanity for the manifestation of the hierarchies of Divine Ones who have charge of the ushering in of the coming New Age through which They can reach the minds and hearts of men. But remember that it is not merely repeating the words that brings the power, but repeating them with all the aspiration and spiritual power implanted in us by Eternal Being in the beginning. It is not lip-service the Holy Ones ask of us, but sincere effort and understanding prayer.

Pause after each sentence and meditate upon it, visualizing its radiance going out to all mankind, consuming all evil and stimulating all good. For it is only through softening the hearts of mankind, through the spread of the warmth of Divine Love and the power of the Living Christ, that *the evil can be overcome and these days be shortened.*

INDEX

THE END

DO YOU LIKE MYSTERIES OF HUMANKIND SUCH AS PROPHECIES OR LEGENDS?

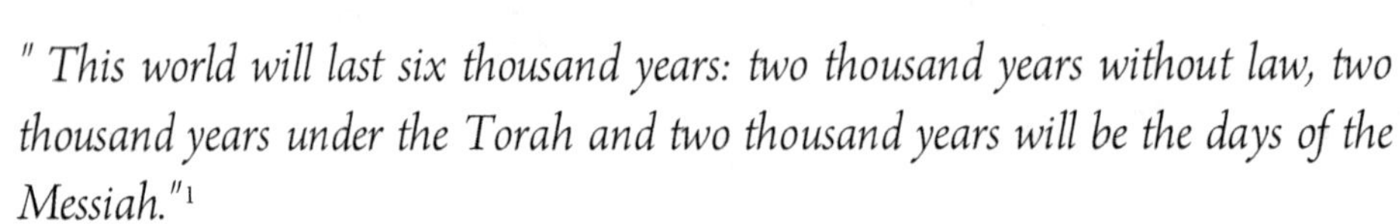

" This world will last six thousand years: two thousand years without law, two thousand years under the Torah and two thousand years will be the days of the Messiah."[1]

[1] This 3 thousand year old prophecy is attributed to Tanna debe Eliyyahu. The 2 thousand years without law are the years from the biblical creation to Abraham. According to Historians and the tradition, Abraham left the Sumerian Ur about 2000 BC. Since then until Christ, more 2 thousand years passed, which are the years under the Torah. From Christ the Messiah to our time, more 2 thousand years were counted. This prophecy is clear: We are near the end of the world.

In the book Global Warming, Global Flood, you will find the following found in some versions of the Corpus Hermeticum, which was not included in this version here. The author, Historian, says:

I found this prophecy in a printed version of the *Corpus Hermeticum*, but I've seen versions without it. The *Corpus Hermeticum* is an old book and very well-known all over the world, mainly for people with some esoteric or occult knowledge. It seems that the *Corpus Hermeticum's* text was written between 2nd century BC and 3rd century AD. The text consists of a set of writings that arrived to us in Greek. The Latin translation of the text, done by Marsilio Ficino, was as incunable[2], printed for the first time in 1471. Later it was translated into other languages. And later, in other editions, the *Corpus Hermeticum* received additions. This work was attributed to mythical Hermes Trismegistus (meaning "Hermes three times big"). This text had a certain importance in the first centuries of the Church and it was popular until the Middle Ages, having inspired hermetic writings which started to bloom at that time. In the end of the 17th century, some writers stated that this text was a fake. This hypothesis had to be totally denied when *Corpus Hermeticum* manuscripts were found in 1945 in *Nag Hammadi*, Egypt, in Coptic, which was the last phase of the Egyptian language, and was spoken by the Christians in Egypt in the first centuries.[3] This very old text has some interesting prophecies, located in the final part of the work. It predicts a flood, which will be a divine instrument for a recreation:

"The earth will lose its balance then, the sea will stop being navigable, the sky won't be full of stars, the stars will stop their march through the sky, all divine voice will be forced to silence and they will remain silent, the fruits of the earth will rot, the soil will stop being fertile, the air will get ill in a dismal torpor. This will happen because of the old age of the world: irreligion, disorder, and irrational confusion in everything. When these things happen, oh Asclepius, then the Lord

[2] Printed before 1500.

[3] According to Athanasius Kircher (1602-1680), an important German Jesuit scholar, Hermes Trismegistus was Moses.

and the Father, the God first in power... will annihilate all the malice, destroying it through a flood, consuming it through the fire, killing it through pestilential illnesses extended to several places, but soon it will drive the world to its beauty as it was in the beginning, so that this same world becomes again worthy of reverence and admiration and so that also God, creator and restorer of such a big work, be glorified by men so that they live, then, with continuous praise, hymns and blessings. In reality, in this moment it will be the birth of the world: a renewal for the good things, a sacred and solemn restoration of the nature, imposed by force as time goes by (...) One day will come when the man will prefer to produce the food with their hands, but the food will be poison. Man will poison the earth, the water and the sky and it will end up also poisoning his heart... A scythe will harvest the victims and a hammer will knead the men."

www.ingramcontent.com/pod-product-compliance
Lightning Source LLC
LaVergne TN
LVHW010930110826
845149LV00013B/2539

* 9 7 8 8 5 6 2 0 2 2 0 7 4 *